T5-CRP-909

WITHDRAWN

PROPERTY OF
ONONDAGA COUNTY PUBLIC LIBRARY
"Whoever wilfully detains any . . . property
belonging to any public or incorporated library . . .
for thirty days after notice in writing to return the
same . . . shall be punished by a fine not less than
one nor more than twenty-five dollars, or by im-
prisonment in jail not exceeding six months . . ."
N Y S Education Law
Section 265

WHITE BRANCH
Onondaga County
Public Library
763 BUTTERNUT STREET
SYRACUSE. NY 13208

11/18/94
THE MISSION FURNITU\ STICKLEY
(1) 1989 # 745.214 MIS

Oak china closet from the Onandaga Shops of L. & J. G. Stickley, circa 1905. Signed with decal. From the collection of Stephen Gray.

THE MISSION FURNITURE OF
L·&·J·G·STICKLEY

Edited by
Stephen Gray

Revised Edition
copyright © 1989
ISBN: 940326-12-4

Published by
TURN of the CENTURY EDITIONS

250 West Broadway
New York, N.Y. 10013

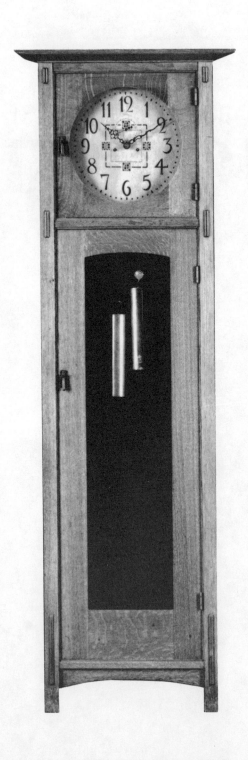

Oak tall case clock by the firm of L. & J. G. Stickly, circa 1908 with red decal.
Photograph courtesy of Nancy A. McClelland, Christie's, New York.

CONTENTS

*Oak cellarette from the Onandaga Shops of L. & J. G. Stickley, circa 1905. Signed
with decal. From the collection of Stephen Gray.*

HISTORY

The L. and J. G. Stickley Furniture Company produced a wide variety of "mission furniture," much of it representing the best aspects of the Arts and Crafts Movement in the United States in terms of structural honesty, simplicity of design and high quality of design. Regrettably, little is known about the design philosophy behind the furniture produced by the company during the early years of the twentieth century because its catalogues contain only brief statements about the designs. Thus, we are left with illustrations in L. and J. G. Stickley catalogues and actual examples of their work as the only evidence of their design intentions and their important position within the Arts and Crafts Movement.

In 1902, the L. and J. G. Stickley Furniture Company began operations in Fayetteville, a small village near Syracuse, New York. The two owners of the new firm, Leopold (1869-1957) who was always called Lee, and John George (1871-1921) were younger brothers of Gustav Stickley who manufactured his Craftsman "mission furniture" in nearby Eastwood. Lee Stickley had been trained in Gustav's factory where he served as foreman from 1899-1901. J. George had been associated with another furniture making brother, Albert Stickley of the Stickley Brothers Company in Grand Rapids, Michigan. Thus, L. and J. G. Stickley were carrying on a family tradition (and competition) when they purchased the Collin, Sisson and Pratt Factory in Fayetteville.

First called the Onondaga Shops after the county in which it was located, the L. and J. G. Stickley Company was incorporated in 1904. The brothers must have been fairly successful from the start however since they bought a number of adjacent pieces of property to expand their operations during the early years. In January 1905, L. and J. G. Stickley presented their "Arts and Crafts and Simple Furniture Built on Mission Lines" to the trade at the annual Grand rapids Furniture Exhibition. Three months later, in March 1905, they published their first catalogue, "Some Sketches of Furniture from the Onondaga Shops," with many well designed pieces of furniture.

It is not surprising that early Onondaga Shops furniture is similar, and in some cases nearly identical, to the Craftsman mission furniture manufactured by their brother. Lee Stickley, earlier Gustav's foreman, surely knew Craftsman methods of furniture construction and the design process involved in creating Craftsman pieces. More importantly, Lee had probably assimilated the philosophy of the Arts and Crafts Movement while working for his brother along with common design inspiration from England.

Unlike Gustav Stickley who published frequent Craftsman furniture catalogues with prices, L. and J. G. Stickley seem to have waited five years before issuing their next catalogue in 1910. In the new catalogue, the Onondaga Shops label was replaced by a new identification with a handscrew shop mark and the words "L. and J. G. Stickley, Handcraft." In keeping with Arts and Crafts precepts, their "plain yet distinctive" furniture was described in terms of "honesty and durability," "simplicity and restfulness." The large catalogue illustrated hundreds of pieces of mission furniture. An innovation of the 1910 furniture was the use of spring cushion seats "original with us so far as furniture is concerned."

"The Works of L. and J. G. Stickley," a 1912 supplement to the 1910 catalogue announced that the handscrew shop mark and the word "Handcraft" would no longer be used to identify their furniture. Surely "Handcraft," so similar to "Craftsman," and the handscrew label, so similar to Gustav Stickley's joiner's compass label, must have caused confusion on the part of potential customers who wanted to buy Stickley furniture. To add to the confusion, there were the two additional Stickley firms, one in Grand Rapids (Albert) and the other in Binghamton, New York (Charles). Henceforth, Fayetteville Stickley furniture was to be labeled "The Work of L. and J. G. Stickley."

L. and J. G. Stickley continued to produce "mission oak furniture" into the early 1920's long after the heyday of the Arts & Crafts movement. After Gustav Stickley went bankrupt, he was associated with L. and J. G. Stickley for a few months; this association was short lived. Leopold Stickley stopped producing Arts and Crafts furniture in 1923, introducing a new style of furniture called "Cherry Valley" which was inspired by American colonial and European prototypes. Although no longer owned by Stickleys, the firm of L. and J. G. Stickley is still in operation today and the high standard of construction present in its earliest furniture continues.

Dr. Mary Ann Clegg Smith
June 1982

PHILOSOPHY
AND CONSTRUCTION

Construction technique at the L. & J. G. Stickley factories during the years it was evolving from the Onondaga Shops does not seem to have been standardized. As in the early perhaps experimental production of the Gustav Stickley factory, details of construction often varied from one piece to the next of any given design. Drawer pulls on early case pieces took the form of crisply faceted rectangular wooden knobs. Metal escutcheons were sometimes fastened with square headed screws and hardware in general could be found in brass as well as the copper that later became standard. Legs on early furniture were sometimes of solid wood and sometimes built up with a sandwich-like lamination. The sides of drawers were sometimes held together with dovetails hand shaped in the English tradition while others were fastened without dovetails. A range of stains, from almost black to natural, was more frequently used and the later preference for "quarter sawed" oak was less evident.

By the time the circa 1905 catalogue appeared, the company was willing to forego any pretense toward Arts and Crafts adherence to a medieval kind of handcraft and opted for "a scientific manner (that) does not attempt to follow the traditions of a bygone day." This approach may well have contributed to the company's longevity and it certainly removed their production from the restricted and ephemeral realm of a philosophical trend to allow them to continue making "mission oak" well into the 20's. Though many designs still carried appendix-like vestiges of Arts and Crafts theory such as loose wedge pinned mortise and tenon joints that appeared in non-functional situations on case pieces, the company's directors were sensitive enough to realize the advantages of adapting to machine production. The almost trademark use of four interlocking pieces of wood around a central core for furniture legs became standard. The claim was that this joinery was superior in strength and durability because it circumscribed the use of veneers and was made of solid wood. More practically, it allowed smaller sections of wood to be utilized and the precision machine cuts eliminated the time consuming dual process of laminating and veneering. Efficiency also required machines to produce the characteristic splined joint that became standard on L. & J. G. Stickley table tops. This spline was decorative as claimed and somewhat more durable than a butt or tongue-and-groove joint which are dependent to a greater degree on glue but it did not prevent splitting as the catalogue implied it would.

Examination of labeled L. & J. G. Stickley furniture reveals that quarter sawn oak was not used consistently even after production became more standardized. The "fine silver flake of the quartering" was certainly appreciated by the manufacturers but they obviously did not see this elaborate grain pattern as essential to the enrichment of their designs. The oak was generally fumed and the customer was encouraged to select a color of finish most suited to his individual taste but the majority of extant L. & J. G. Stickley pieces retaining original finish are in the standard medium brown factory finish. As previously noted, dark finishes do appear on some early pieces and some custom stains such as the then popular green are known.

The work of L. & J. G. Stickley can often be identified by the most obvious details of joinery. The loose wedge pins are usually shaped with a faceted rather than curved outline, the latter being more typical of Craftsman furniture. The table top spline is more precise than those found on Limbert Arts and Crafts furniture. Designs of the L. & J. G. Stickley factory seldom approach the degree of European sophistication that was evident in Limbert's production yet neither do they depend on constructional theories as many of Gustav Stickley's seemed to. The catalogue's claim that this was "entirely American" furniture may have been an overstatement. Many ideas used by L. & J. G. Stickley were "second generation" having been interpreted earlier by Gustav Stickley from such British designers as C.F.A. Voysey and H.M. Baillie Scott. The concept of honest construction through handwork was no longer revolutionary, it was, in fact, so firmly established that the Stickley's were free to use machines to state the idea symbolically.

Robert L. Edwards
September 1982

THE ONONDAGA SHOPS

Leopold and John George Stickley manufactured their "Arts and Crafts furniture built on Mission lines" under the Onondaga Shops label starting in 1902. The catalogue shown here was published in 1905. The sketches following are from a bound portfolio probably issued during that same period. Some of the furniture designs are illustrated in similar or modified forms in both sections. These designs were refined and appear in the later, more elaborate catalogues. The sketches depict the early copper hardware and faceted rectangular wooden pulls. Laced seams on the leather cushions were also typical of this period. Even though the drawings were done in a crude fashion the actual pieces were expertly crafted and represent some of the best work of L. & J. G. Stickley.

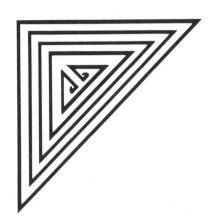

HANDMADE FURNITURE
FROM THE

ONONDAGA SHOPS
L. & J. G. STICKLEY
INC.
FAYETTEVILLE, NEW YORK

THE FOLLOWING PAGES OF DESIGNS ARE A FEW OF OUR LATEST PRODUCTIONS, TO WHICH WE ARE CONTINUALLY ADDING

THE SKETCHES HAVE BEEN CARE-FULLY MADE AND CUSTOMERS CAN RELY UPON AN ACCURATE REPRESENTATION AS TO WHAT THE GOODS ARE

THIS FURNITURE IS MADE IN CARE-FULLY SELECTED OAK, WITH A DULL WAX FINISH

SAMPLES OF THE DIFFERENT FIN-ISHES OF BOTH WOOD AND LEATHER WILL BE PROMPTLY SENT ON REQUEST

ONONDAGA SHOPS
L. & J. G. STICKLEY, Inc.
FAYETTEVILLE
NEW YORK

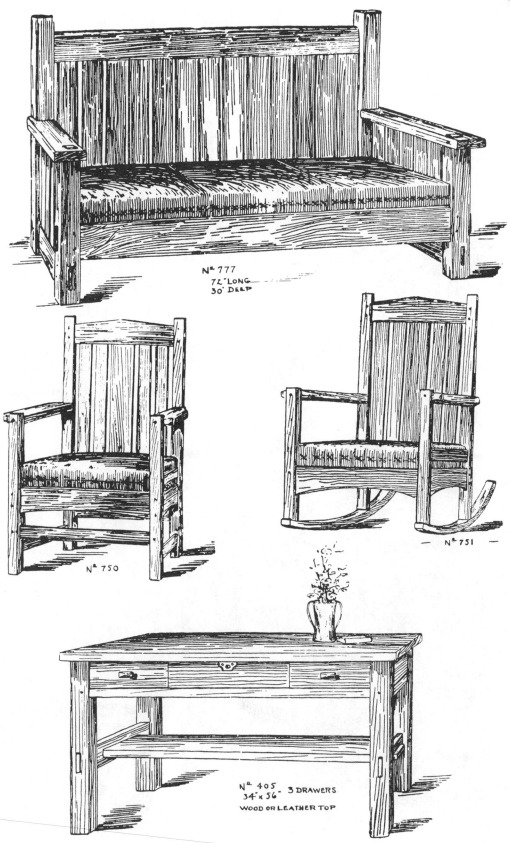

Nº 777
72" LONG
30" DEEP

Nº 750

Nº 751

Nº 405 - 3 DRAWERS
34" x 56"
WOOD OR LEATHER TOP

Nº 774

Nº 326 OPEN. HIGH. 56. Nº 326½ CLOSED.
WIDE 30.
DEEP 12"

Nº 121
64" HIGH.
PANELS 16" WIDE

Nº 311.
20"x17"
16" HIGH

Nª 763

Nª 345
45" HIGH
19" WIDE

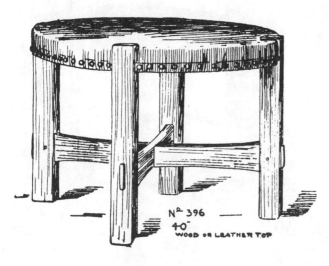

Nª 396
40"
WOOD OR LEATHER TOP

Nª 764A

Nº 125.
70"HIGH
PANELS 23" WIDE

Nº 784

Nº 775.   With Panels.
84" LONG
32" DEEP

Nº 402
22"x40"

Nº 756

Nº 757

Nº 388
36"

Nº 770

Nº 331
70 LONG
56 HIGH

Nº 776

Nº 325
13 TOP
22 HIGH

Nº 404
22"x40"

27"x34"
GLASS 16"x26"
N° 65

N° 741
40" LONG
24" DEEP

N° 752

N° 753

N° 375
28"x42"

N° 782

N° 310

N° 783

N° 327 OPEN - HIGH 56". N° 327 CLOSED.
WIDE 36"
DEEP 12"

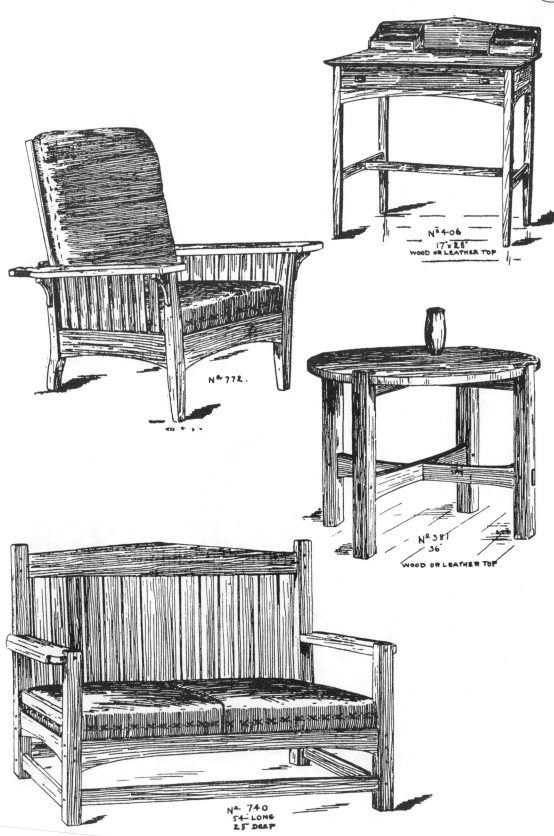

Nº 406
17"x 28"
WOOD OR LEATHER TOP

Nº 772.

Nº 381
36"
WOOD OR LEATHER TOP

Nº 740
54" LONG
25" DEEP

Nº 401
19" x 34"

Nº 764

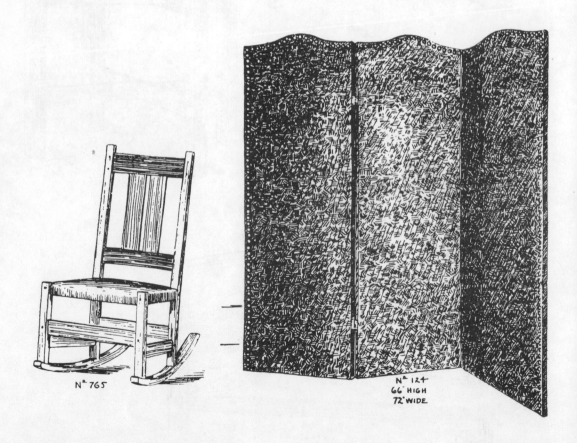

Nº 765

Nº 124
66" HIGH
72" WIDE

Nº 751½

Nº 505
33" HIGH
TOP 13" & 27"

Nº 387.
16"

Nº 509
TOP 16"
20" HIGH

Nº 750½

Nº 403
48" LONG
26" DEEP

Nº 767

Nº 766

Nº 739.
76" LONG
30" WIDE

Nº 758

Nº 397
28"x40"

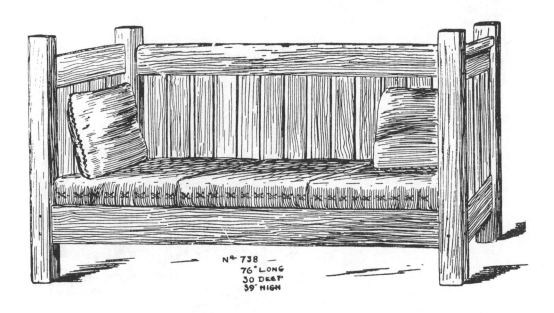

Nº 738
76" LONG
30 DEEP
39" HIGH

Nº 394.
45" x 72

Nº 386
30"

Nº 760

Nº 761

Nº 780

Nº 384
48" & 54"
WOOD OR LEATHER TOP

Nº 346
42" HIGH
21" WIDE

Nº 781

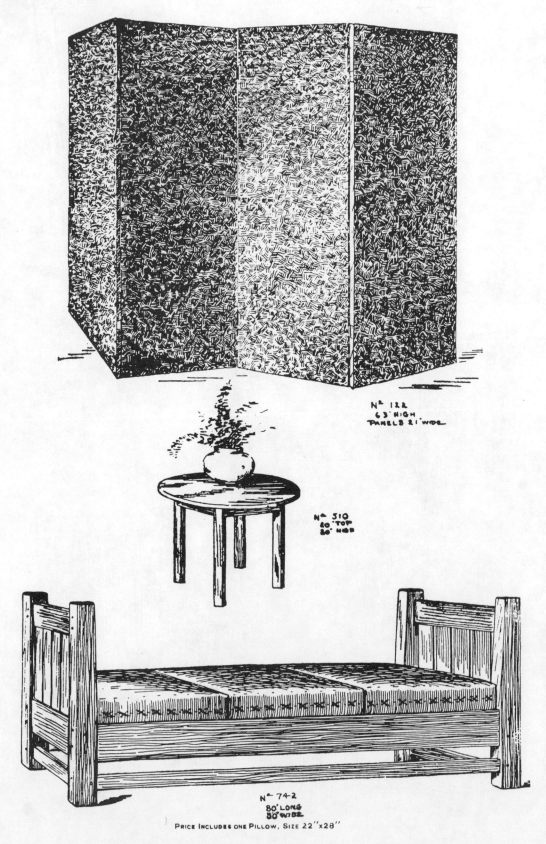

Nº 122
63" HIGH
PANELS 21" WIDE

Nº 510
40" TOP
30" HIGH

Nº 742
80" LONG
30" WIDE
PRICE INCLUDES ONE PILLOW, SIZE 22"x28"

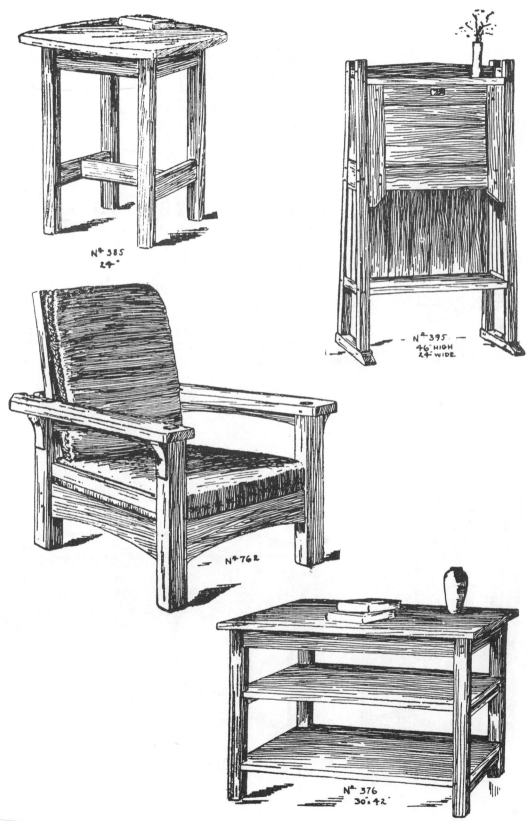

Nᵈ 385
24"

Nᵈ 395
46" HIGH
24" WIDE

Nᵈ 762

Nᵈ 376
30"×42"

Nº 755

Nº 328·OPEN   HIGH 56·   Nº 328½ CLOSED
WIDE 49·
DEEP 12·

Nº 754

Nº 400
26'x42'

Nº 778

Nº 380
30"
WOOD OR LEATHER TOP

Nº 377
30"x48"

Nº 779

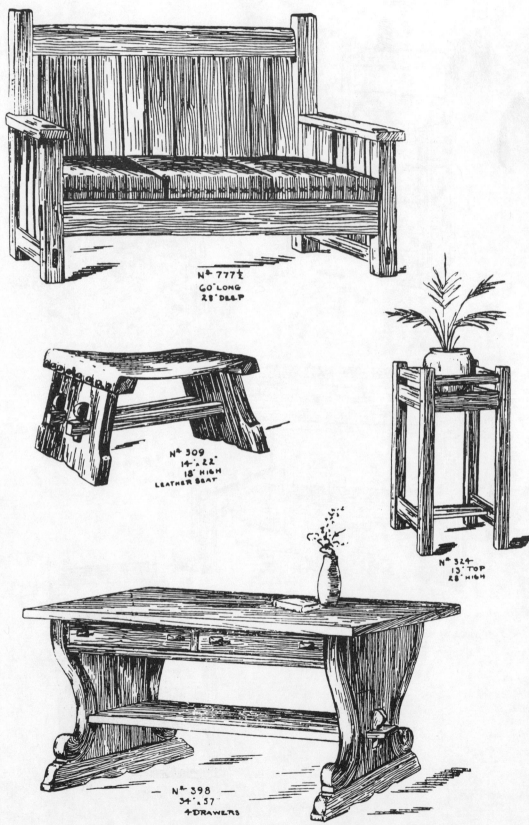

Nº 777½
60″ LONG
28″ DEEP

Nº 309
14″ x 22″
18″ HIGH
LEATHER SEAT

Nº 324
13″ TOP
28″ HIGH

— Nº 398 —
34″ x 57″
4 DRAWERS

Nº 506
20"x 40"

Nº 508
24 TOP
24 HIGH

Nº 399
30 x 48

Nº 379
34"x 56"

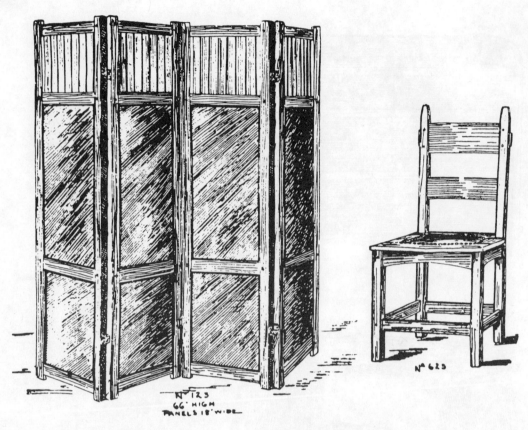

N° 123
66" HIGH
PANELS 18" WIDE

N° 623

N° 624

N° 618

Nº 611

Nº 619
66" HIGH
36" WIDE
14" DEEP

Nº 617
18"x36"

Nº 612

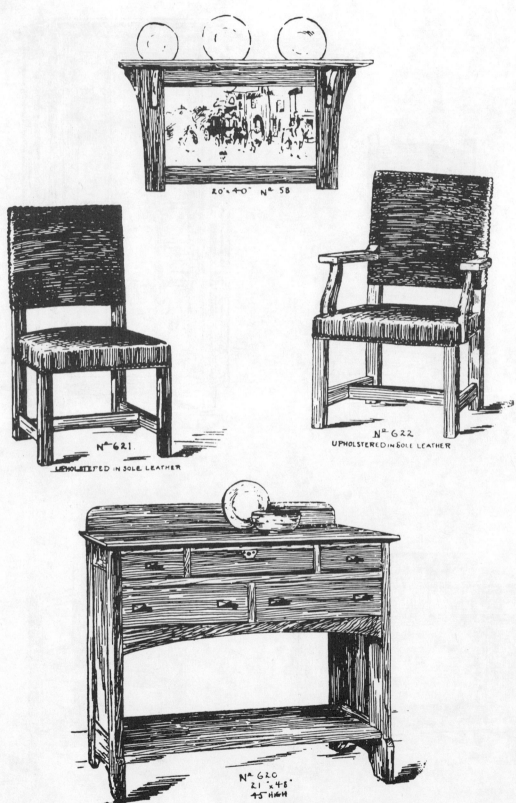

20"x 40" Nº 5B

Nº 621.

UPHOLSTERED IN SOLE LEATHER

Nº 622

UPHOLSTERED IN SOLE LEATHER

Nº 620
21"x 48"
45" HIGH

Nº 788

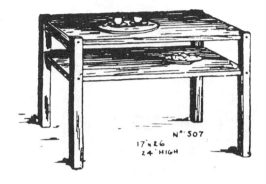

Nº 507
17"x26
24" HIGH

Nº 787

Nº 786

— Nº 792 —

— Nº 791 —

— Nº 793 —

— Nº 794 —

THE ONONDAGA SHOPS

Some Sketches

of

Furniture

Made at The
Onondaga
Shops

THESE SKETCHES ARE INTENDED FOR REFERENCE ONLY. They are offered as evidences of intention, illustrating the story so far as the story can be told by drawings of a small size. The sketches are instruments explanatory of service. It is the *Furniture*, not the drawings, which is presented to the public. The drawings cannot show the texture, color, or even the construction. These must be looked for in the Furniture itself. It has been justly said that all Mission Furniture looks alike: It does—on paper.

A visit to The Onondaga Shops, a glance at the work itself, conveys a different impression. The workers devote their abilities to the making of Furniture which is good, sound, serious, and above all, interesting. They hope to win favor by virtue of practical common sense; the obvious study of proportion and scale; the proper value of plain surfaces contrasted with surfaces slightly carved; and hold that the selection of suitable places for accent is next in importance to construction itself. They realize that wood is peculiarly susceptible to the art and skill of the worker. Some of this Furniture has quaint cuttings in places; some has metal work to accent certain points; some has an outline simple and so devoid of ornament as to be almost severe in its plainness; but all is frankly constructed and the best that they can make.

Realizing that they are servants of the public, they request suggestions of a practical nature which will assist them in making their work more serviceable and beautiful.

THE ONONDAGA SHOPS

L. & J. G. Stickley (Inc.)
Fayetteville, New York, U.S.A.

Nº 712½

Nº 798

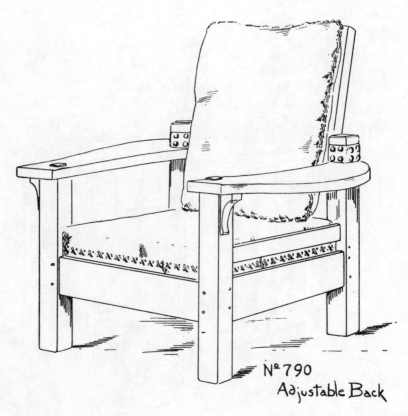

Nº 790
Adjustable Back

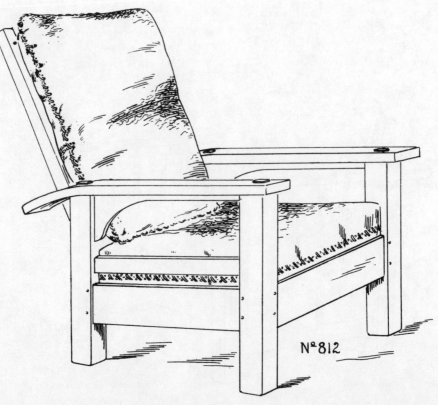

Nº 812

Nº 811

Nº 1121

Mahogany only

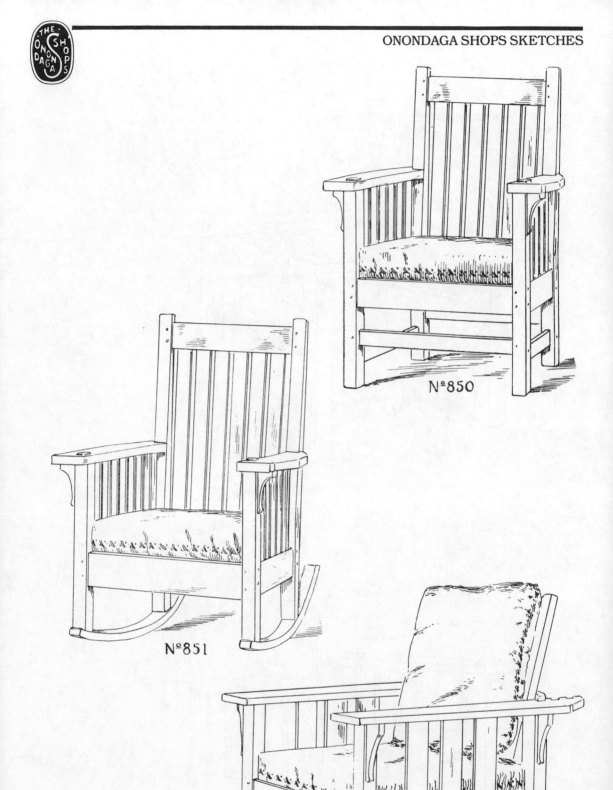

Nº850

Nº851

Nº 768

MORRIS CHAIR
Nº 200

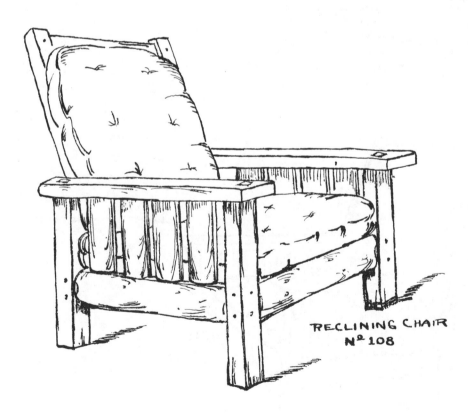

RECLINING CHAIR
Nº 108

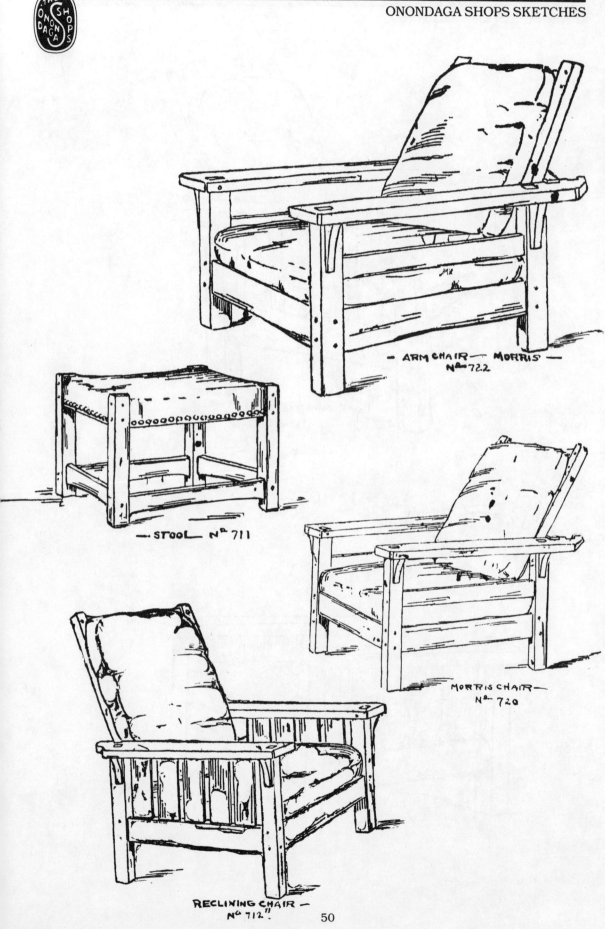

— ARM CHAIR — MORRIS —
Nª 722

— STOOL — Nª 711

MORRIS CHAIR —
Nª 720

RECLINING CHAIR —
Nº 712"

Nº 769

Nº 860

Nº 861

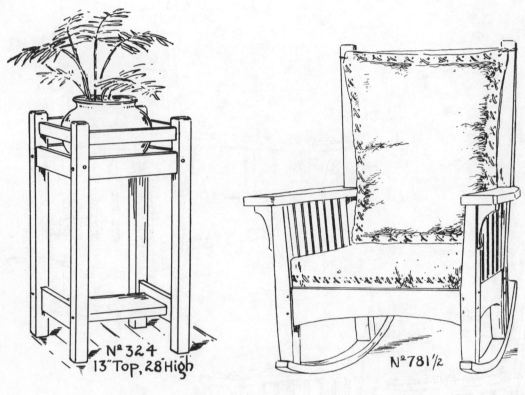

Nº 324
13" Top, 28" High

Nº 781½

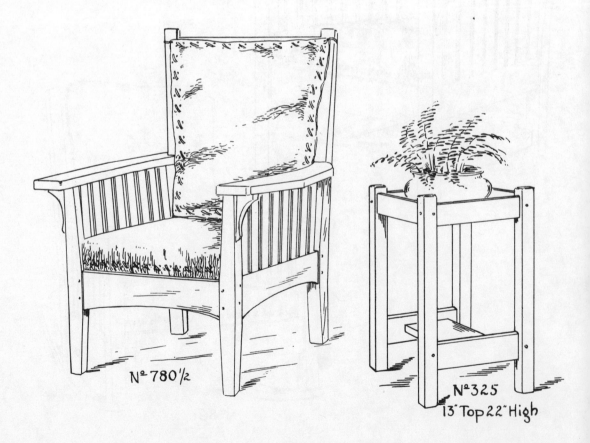

Nº 780½

Nº 325
13" Top 22" High

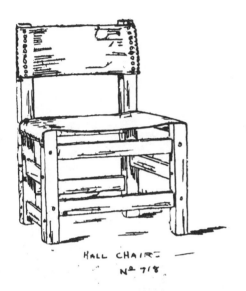

HALL CHAIR
Nº 718

ARM CHAIR
Nº 716

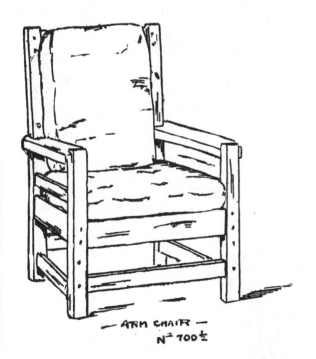

ARM CHAIR
Nº 700½

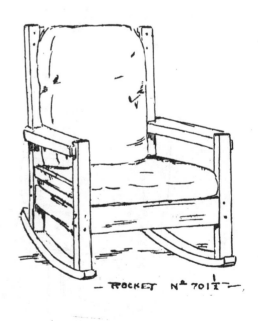

ROCKER Nº 701½

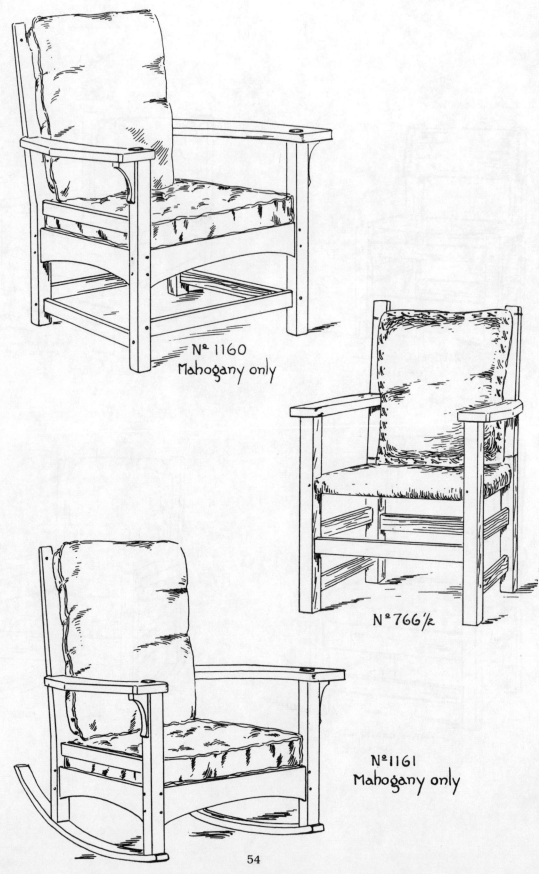

Nº 1160
Mahogany only

Nº 766½

Nº 1161
Mahogany only

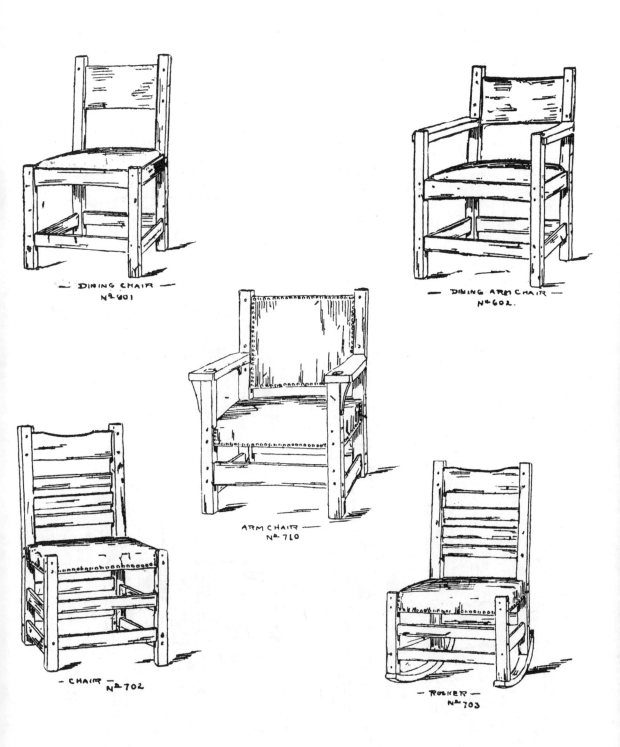

— DINING CHAIR —
Nº 601

— DINING ARM CHAIR —
Nº 602.

ARM CHAIR —
Nº 710

— CHAIR —
Nº 702

— ROCKER —
Nº 703

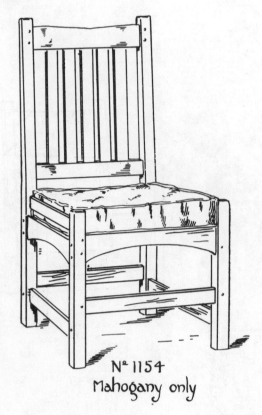

Nº 1154
Mahogany only

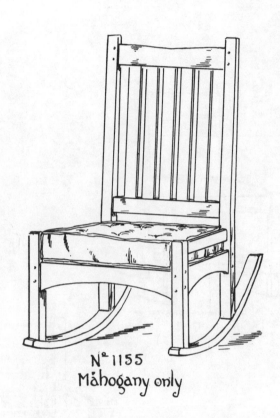

Nº 1155
Mahogany only

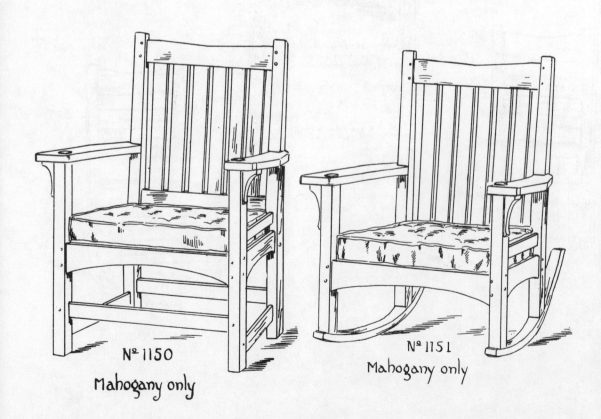

Nº 1150
Mahogany only

Nº 1151
Mahogany only

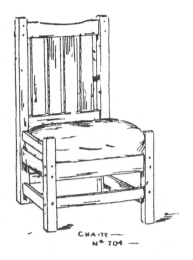

— CHAIR —
Nº 704 —

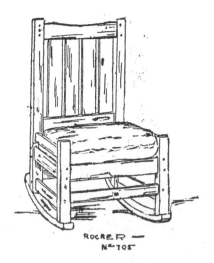

— ROCKER —
Nº 705 —

— ARM CHAIR —
Nº 700 —

— DESK CHAIR —
Nº 714 —

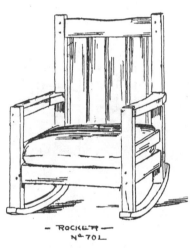

— ROCKER —
Nº 70L

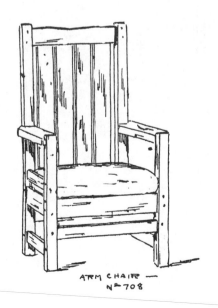

— ARM CHAIR —
Nº 708

— ROCKER —
Nº 709

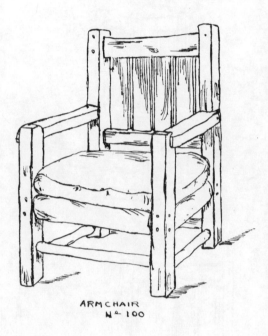

ARM CHAIR
Nº 100

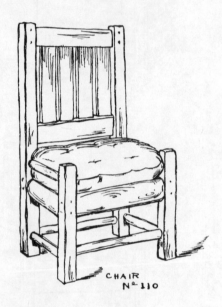

CHAIR
Nº 110

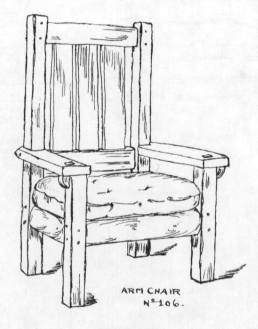

ARM CHAIR
Nº 106.

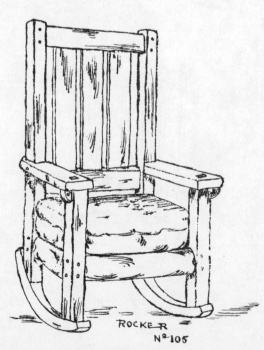

ROCKER
Nº 105

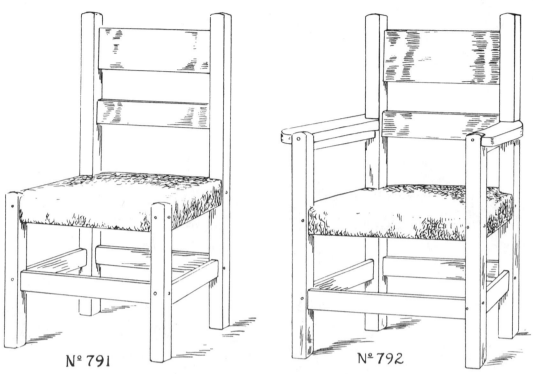

Nº 791

Nº 792

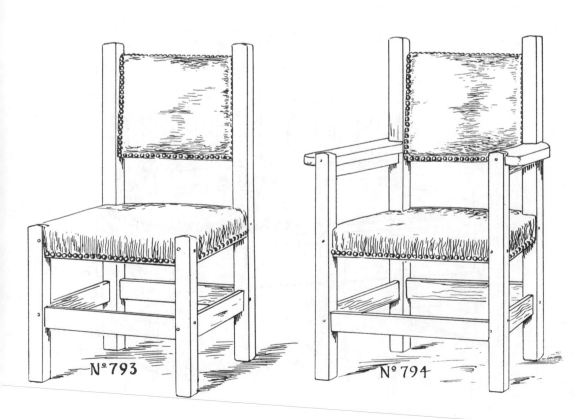

Nº 793

Nº 794

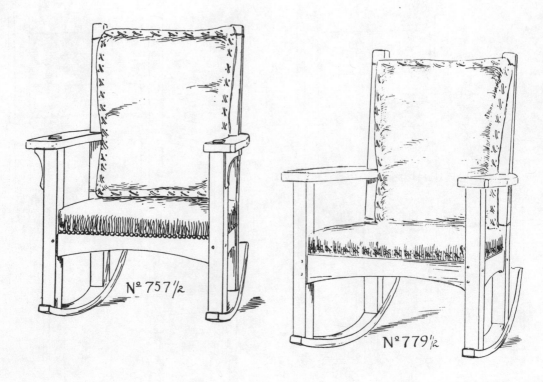

Nº 757½

Nº 779½

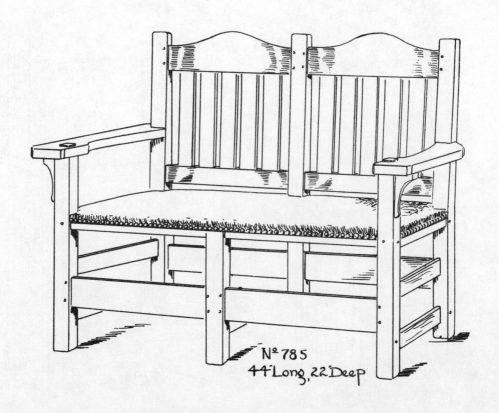

Nº 785
44"Long, 22"Deep

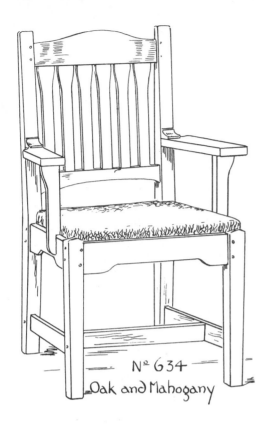

Nº 634
Oak and Mahogany

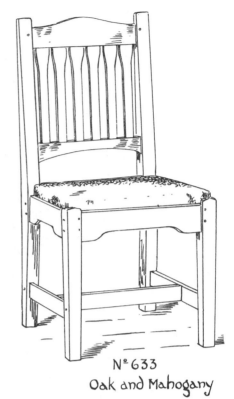

Nº 633
Oak and Mahogany

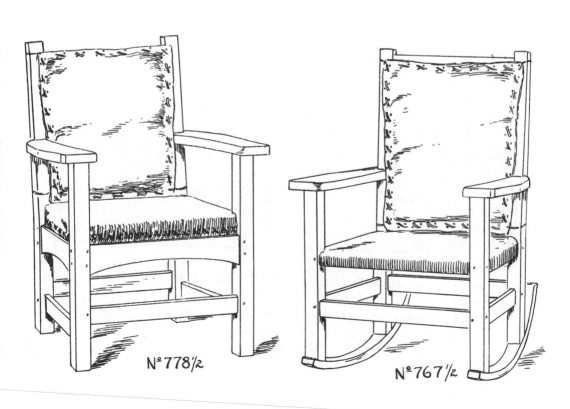

Nº 778½

Nº 767½

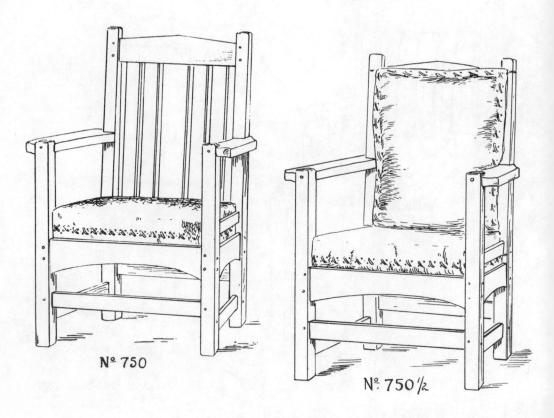

Nº 750

Nº 750½

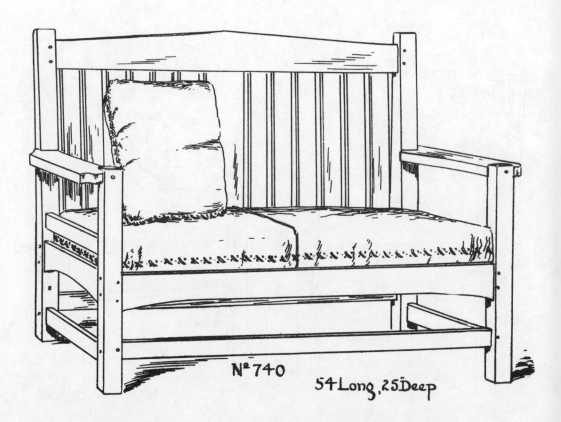

Nº 740

54 Long, 25 Deep

Frame N.º 66   Glass 16"x 30"

N.º 809
37"High, 42"Long, 18"Deep

N.º 626

N.º 625

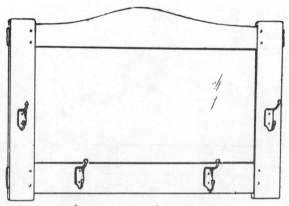

Frame No 65. Glass 18"x 34"

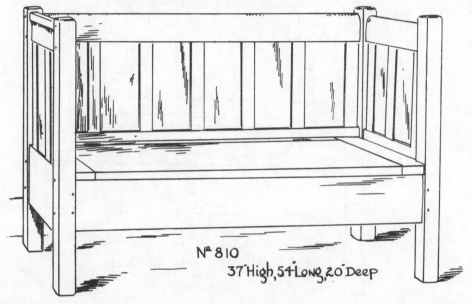

No 810
37"High, 54"Long, 20"Deep

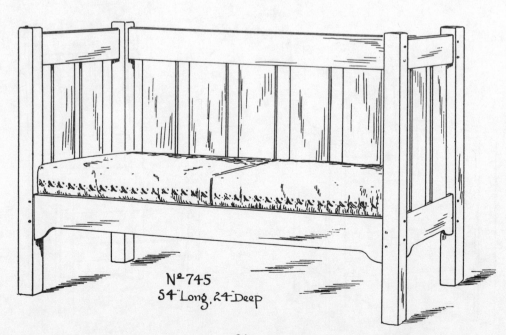

No 745
54"Long, 24"Deep

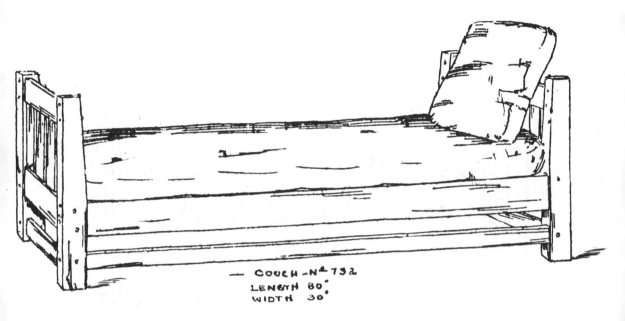

— COUCH - Nº 732
LENGTH 80"
WIDTH 30"

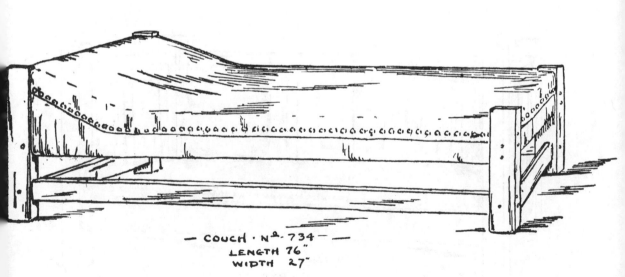

— COUCH · Nº 734 —
LENGTH 76"
WIDTH 27"

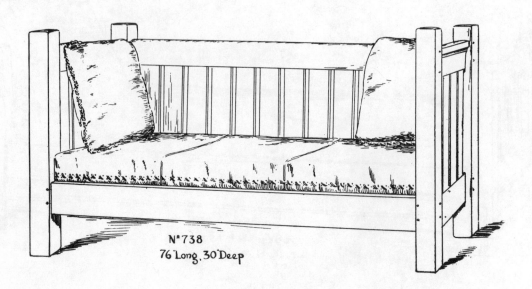

Nº 738
76" Long, 30" Deep

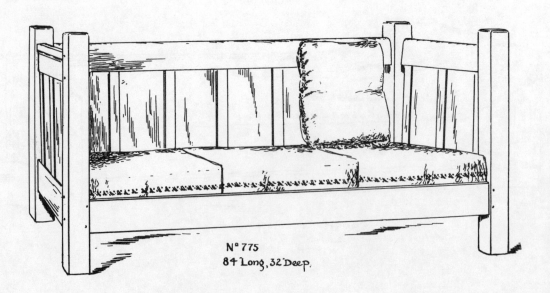

Nº 775
84" Long, 32" Deep.

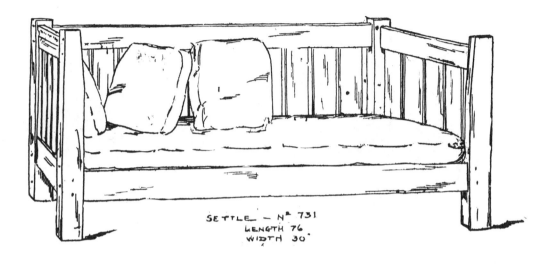

SETTLE — Nº 731
LENGTH 76.
WIDTH 30.

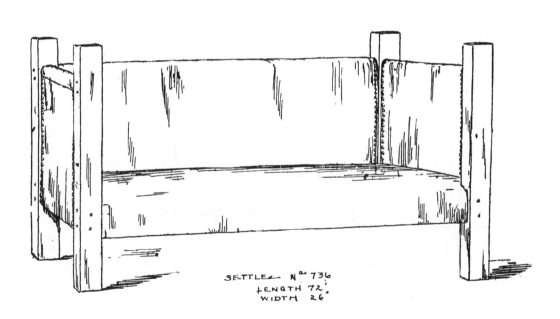

SETTLE Nº 736
LENGTH 72.
WIDTH 26.

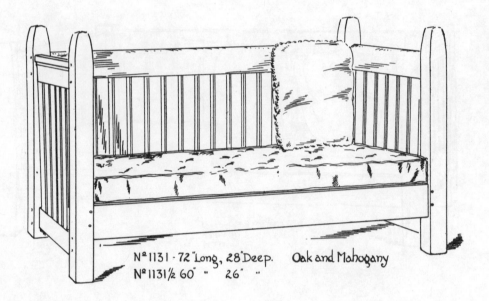

Nº 1131 - 72" Long, 28"Deep.   Oak and Mahogany
Nº 1131½ 60" "   26"   "

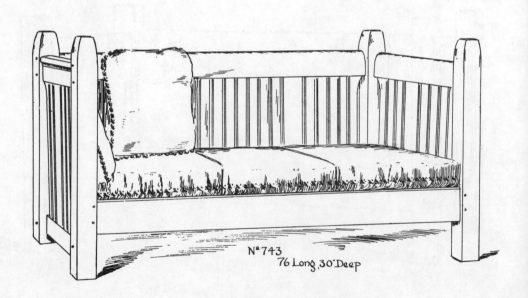

Nº 743
76 Long, 30"Deep

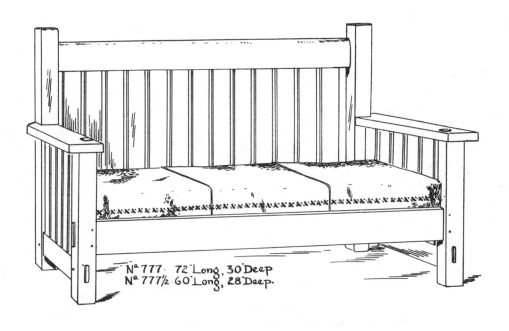

Nº 777 · 72" Long, 30"Deep
Nº 777½ 60"Long, 28"Deep.

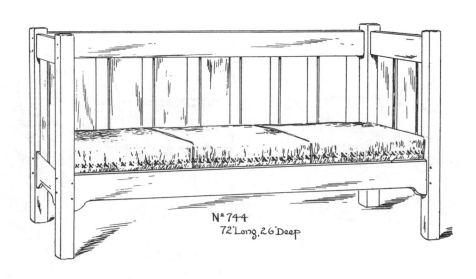

Nº 744
72"Long, 26"Deep

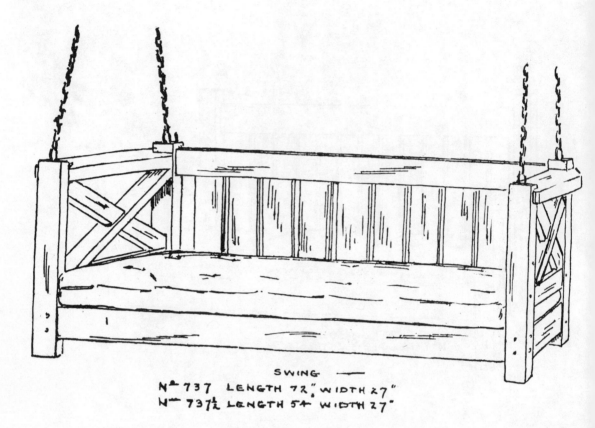

SWING

Nº 737 LENGTH 72" WIDTH 27"

Nº 737½ LENGTH 54" WIDTH 27"

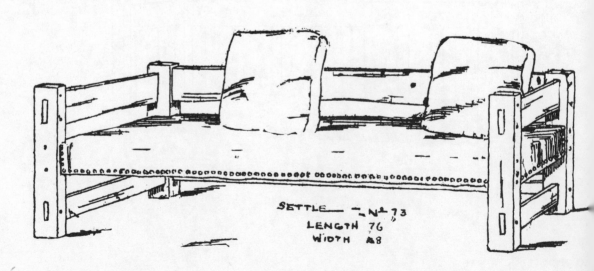

SETTLE — Nº 73

LENGTH 76"

WIDTH 28

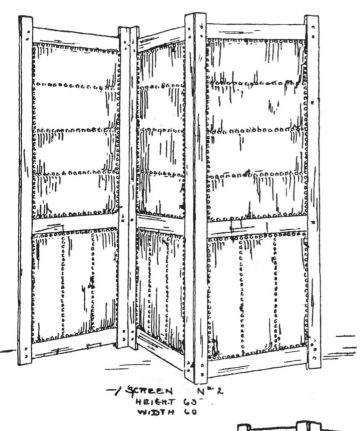

—/ SCREEN   Nº 2
HEIGHT 65"
WIDTH 60

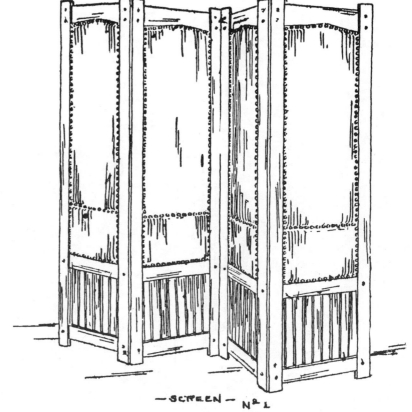

— SCREEN — Nº 1
HEIGHT 66".1
WIDTH 64".1

Nº 741
40"Long, 24 Deep

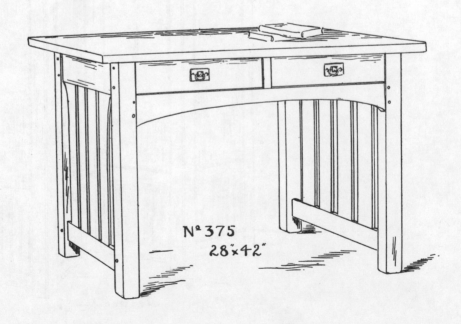

Nº 375
28"x 42"

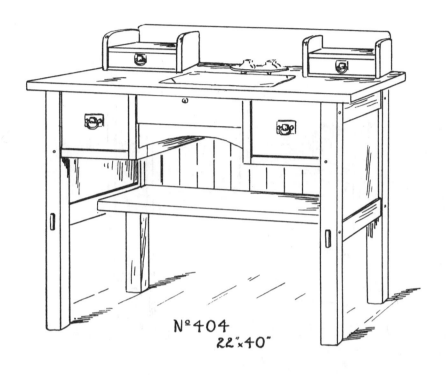

Nº 404
22"×40"

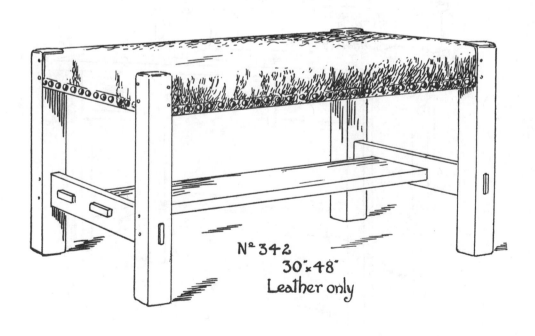

Nº 342
30"×48"
Leather only

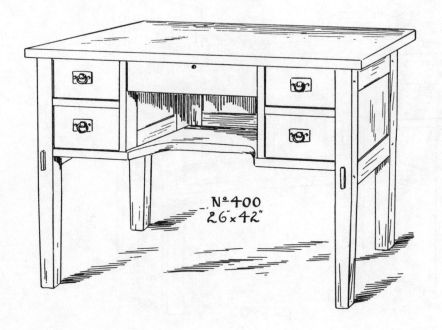

Nº 400
26"x42"

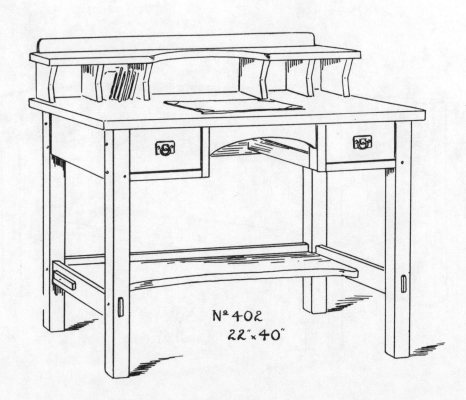

Nº 402
22"x40"

Nº 401
20"×34"

Nº 799

Nº 345
45" High, 19" Wide

Nº 406
17"×28"

N⁰ 326 Open. N⁰ 326½ Closed
56" High, 30" Wide, 12" Deep

N⁰ 327 Open. N⁰ 327½ Closed
56" High, 36" Wide, 12" Deep

Nº 328 Open   Nº 328½ Closed.
56″ High, 49″ Wide, 12″ Deep

Nº 331-OPEN
Nº 331½-CLOSED   56″ HIGH, 70″ WIDE 12″ DEEP

BOOK SHELVES —
WITH CABINET Nº 320
HEIGHT 42"
WIDTH. 30"

HANGING BOOK CABINET — Nº 321
LENGTH 4-0
HEIGHT 18"

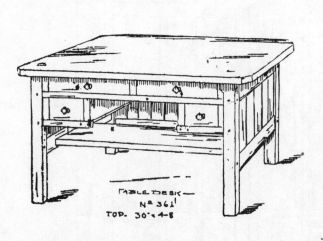

TABLE DESK —
Nº 361
TOP. 30"x 4-8

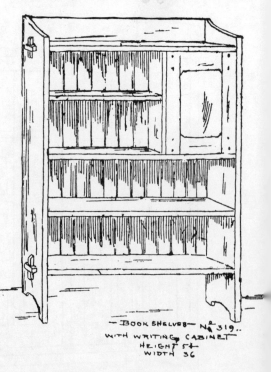

— BOOK SHELVES — Nº 319..
WITH WRITING CABINET
HEIGHT 54
WIDTH 36

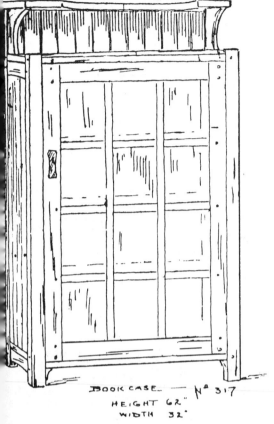

BOOK CASE — Nº 317
HEIGHT 62"
WIDTH 32"

— BOOK CASE —
Nº 318
HEIGHT 55"
WIDTH 32"

— TABLE Nº 351 —
WOOD OR   TOP 36"
LEATHER

DESK — N° 374
HEIGHT 46
WIDTH 24

— DESK N° 370 —
HEIGHT 52"
WIDTH 36"

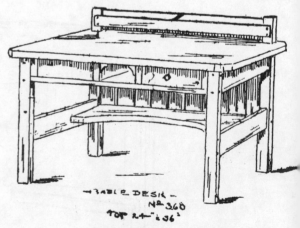

TABLE DESK —
N° 360
TOP 24" x 36"

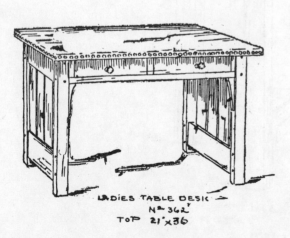

LADIES TABLE DESK →
N° 362
TOP 21"x36"

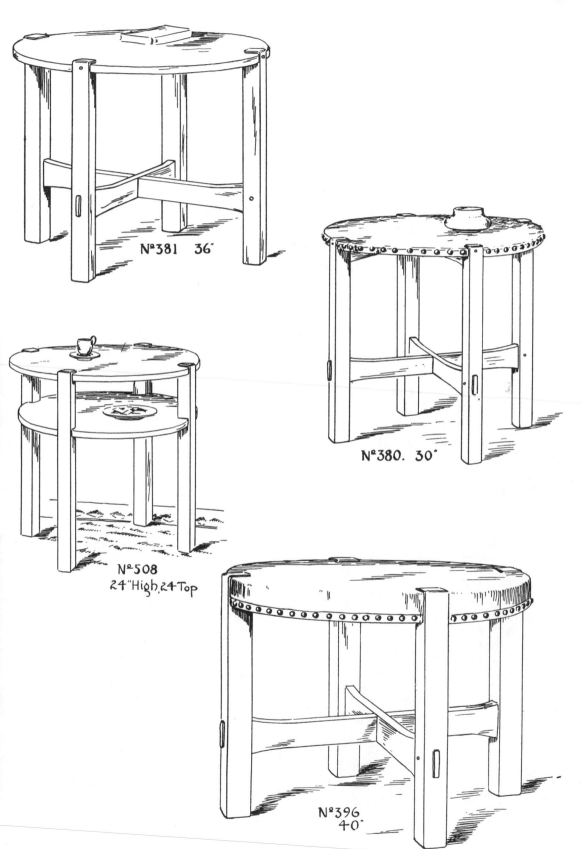

Nº 381   36″

Nº 380.   30″

Nº 508
24″High, 24 Top

Nº 396
40″

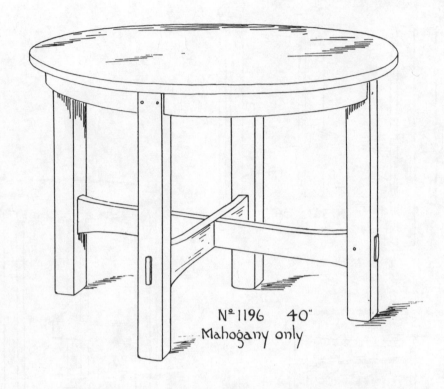

Nº 1196   40"
Mahogany only

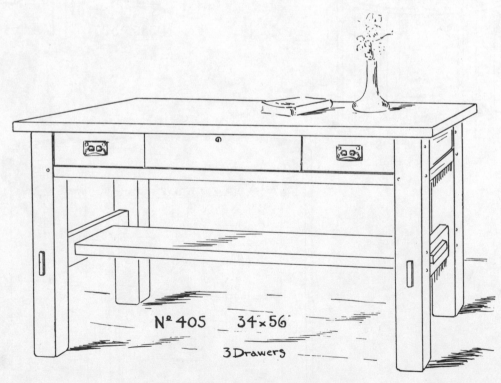

Nº 405   34"x 56"

3 Drawers

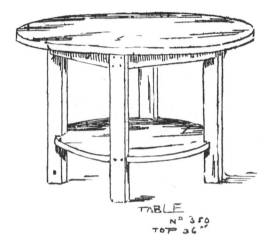

TABLE
Nᵒ 350
TOP 36"

TABLE Nᵒ 350

WOOD
OR
LEATHER

TOP
30"

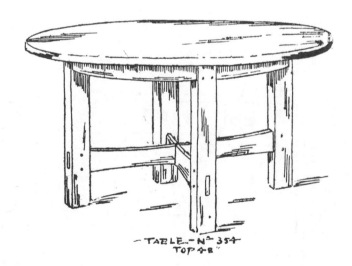

TABLE Nᵒ 354
TOP 48"

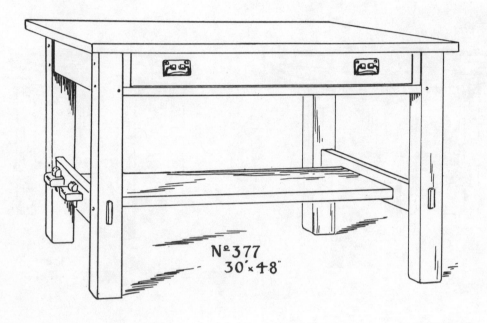

Nº 377
30″×48″

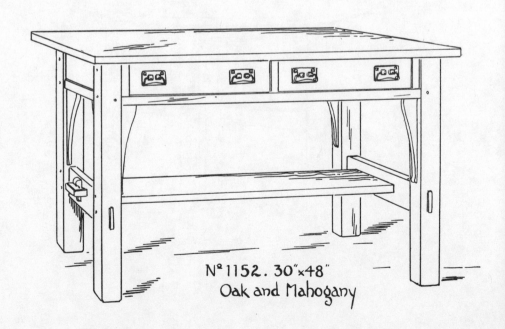

Nº 1152. 30″×48″
Oak and Mahogany

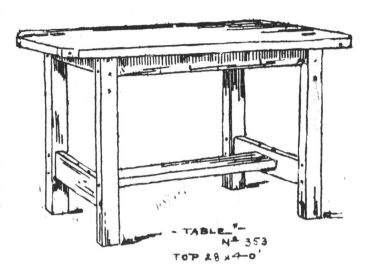

- TABLE -
Nº 353
TOP 28 x 4-0'

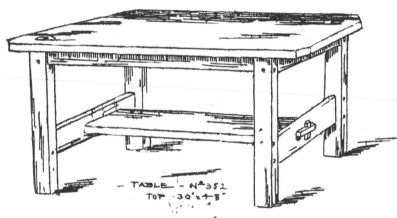

- TABLE - Nº 352
TOP 30"x 4 8"

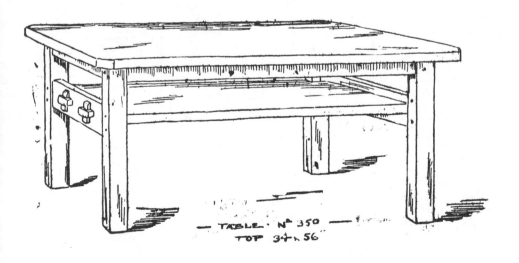

- TABLE - Nº 350
TOP 34 x 56"

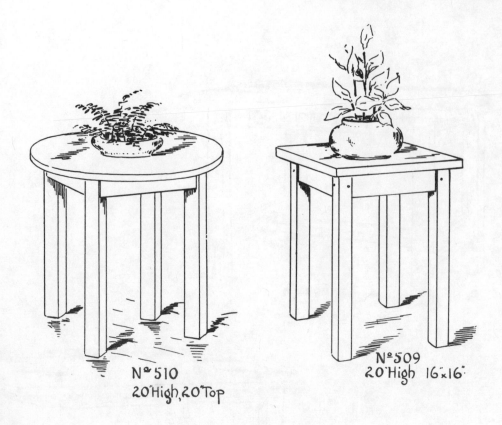

Nº 510
20"High, 20"Top

Nº 509
20"High 16"x16"

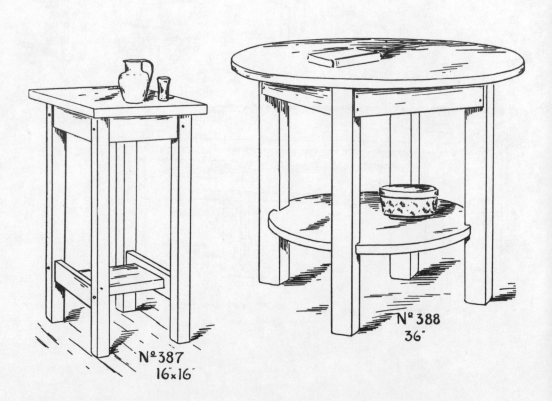

Nº 387
16"x16"

Nº 388
36"

PLANT STAND
No 324

PLANT STAND
No 325

DRINK STAND
No 357

TABLE No 355
TOP 14"

TABLE N-356
TOP 30"

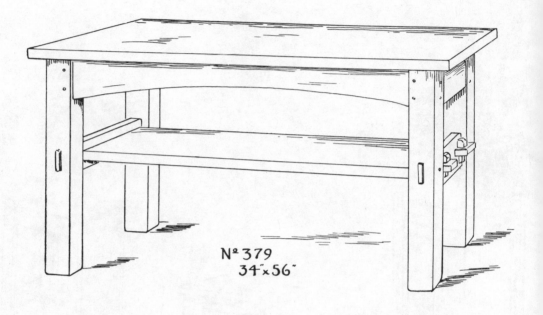

Nº 379
34″×56″

Nº 384
48″ and 54″

Nº376. 30"×42"

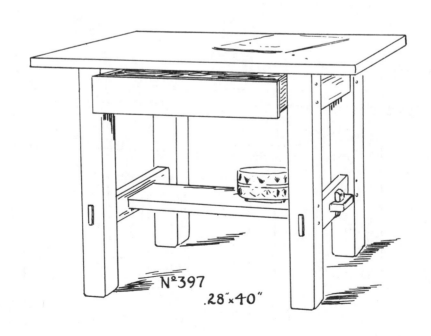

Nº397
.28"×40"

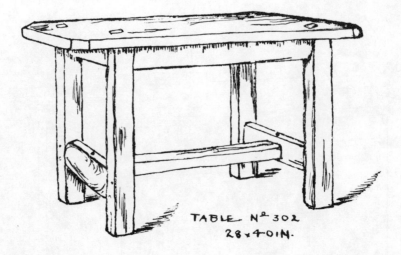

TABLE N.º 302
28 x 40 IN.

TABLE N.º 303
TOP 36 IN.
TABLE N.º 304
40 IN. TOP

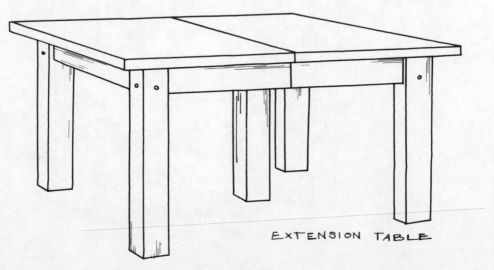

EXTENSION TABLE

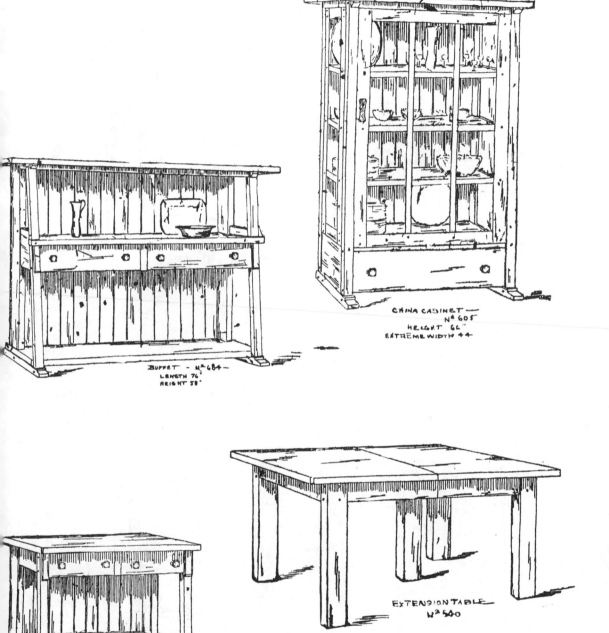

CHINA CABINET
Nº 605
HEIGHT 66"
EXTREME WIDTH 44

BUFFET - Nº 684 -
LENGTH 76"
HEIGHT 58"

SERVING TABLE
Nº 605
LENGTH 36"
WIDTH 18"

EXTENSION TABLE
Nº 540

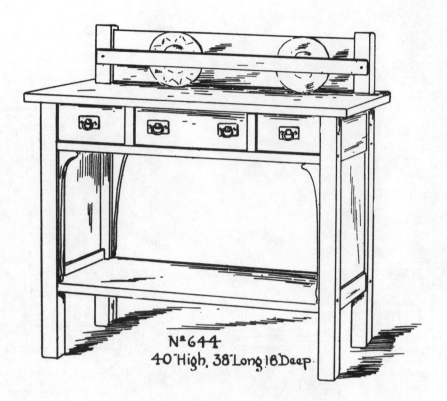

Nº 644
40"High, 38"Long, 18"Deep

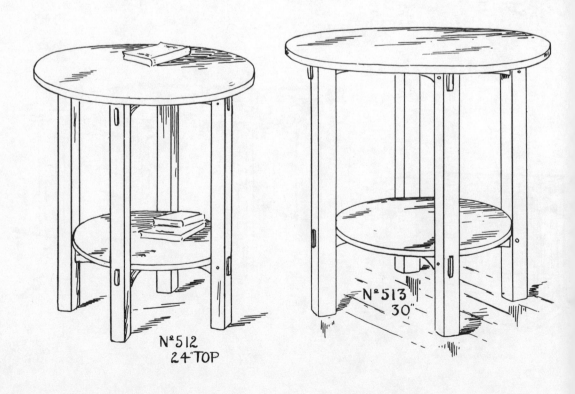

Nº 512
24"TOP

Nº 513
30"

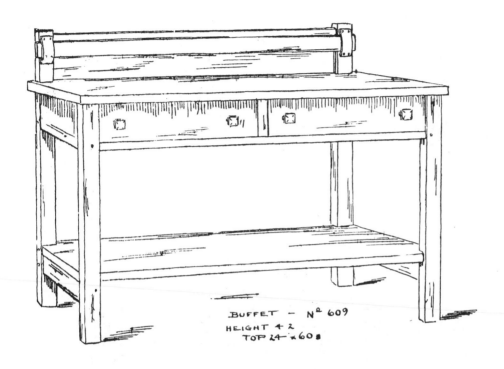

BUFFET — N⁰ 609
HEIGHT 42
TOP 24 x 60 ⁸

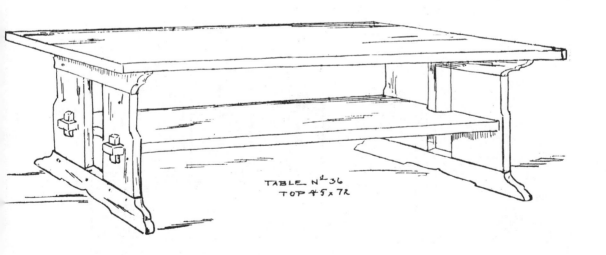

TABLE N⁰ 36
TOP 45 x 72

Nº641
44˝High, 44˝Long, 18˝Deep

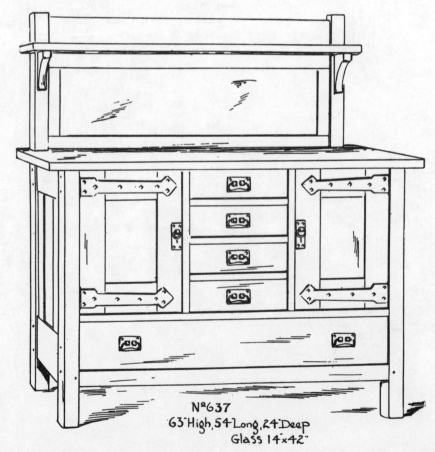

Nº637
63˝High, 54˝Long, 24˝Deep
Glass 14˝x42˝

Nº 640
49 High 48 Long. 22 Deep

Nº 645
52 High. 54 Long. 24 Deep

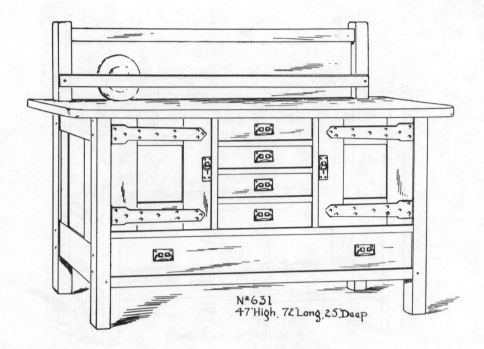

Nº 631
47˝ High, 72˝ Long, 25˝ Deep

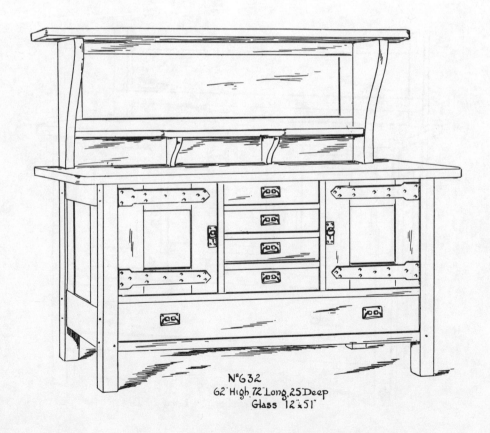

Nº 632
62˝ High, 72˝ Long, 25˝ Deep
Glass 12˝x51˝

Nº 629
70˚High, 47˚Wide, 16˚Deep

Nº 646
70 High, 44 Wide 16 Deep

Nº642
69 High, 51 Wide, 17 Deep

Oak and copper lamp with original woven sea grass shade by the firm of L. & J. G. Stickley. Signed with a white decal. From the collection of Stephen Gray.

THE HANDCRAFT SHOPS

The following section is a compilation of the entire 1910 "Handcraft Furniture of L. & J. G. Stickley" catalogue. We have rearranged all the pages and pictures for easier viewing. The original catalogue was 148 pages and through combination and photographic reduction of illustrations it now only comprises 60 pages of this book. To obtain the best possible result we shot a large portion of the furniture sketches directly from the actual crayon drawings done at the time for L. & J. G. Stickley. The originals were generously loaned to us by Alfred Audi the present owner of the L. & J. G. Stickley Furniture Company of Fayetteville, N.Y.

HANDCRAFT FURNITURE

A Catalogue containing reproductions of
Crayon Drawings of the Furniture
made in the Handcraft Shops,
together with the prin-
cipal dimensions of
each piece

L. & J. G. STICKLEY
FAYETTEVILLE, N. Y., U. S. A.

FOREWORD

I N PUBLISHING this book of Handcraft Furniture, we are considering the present day need for simplicity and restfulness in home surroundings. Built to suit modern conditions and requirements, our furniture appeals to the home-builder in search of plain yet distinctive furnishings. Every piece is designed with a view to its harmonious effect in a modern room, where quiet color-schemes prevail and furniture and walls form an unobtrusive background. The restful lines and beautiful coloring that we give to wood and leather lend a simple friendliness to the products of our shops, and they are eminently in accord with the modern movement towards dignity and harmony in home furnishings.

CONSTRUCTION   In the construction of our furniture we strive for honesty and durability. Our designs show careful study of line and proportion, and comfort is an important consideration. Straight lines are sometimes relieved by graceful curves, but the only ornament lies in structural features that are both useful and decorative, such as pins and tenons. In our chair-arm and post construction, for instance, the tenon which connects the two is an ornamental feature as well as a vital part of the construction. Our excellent workmanship insures durability, and a hundred years of existence can be predicted for each piece of Handcraft Furniture, on account of the care exerted in every detail of its building.

WOOD   The wood employed in our shops is quarter-sawed white oak, chosen because of its strength and its close grained surface, and also for the rich brown color it acquires when subjected to the fumes of ammonia. Oak is fast becoming a rare wood and will soon be as difficult as mahogany to procure in large quantities. We find, however, in the forests of Kentucky a quality of oak well suited to our purpose.

FINISHES   We appreciate the importance of harmonious color in the modern home, and in the years devoted to the making of Handcraft we have given especial attention to the preparation of stains and finishes. Our experiments have resulted in a treatment of oak that brings out its beauties of grain and texture and gives it soft dull tones of nut brown or of forest green. The furniture is subjected in air-tight compartments to the fumes of strong ammonia, which penetrate and color the wood. It is then scraped and sanded, and is further treated with our stains and wax finishes until a smooth, satiny surface is obtained, delightful to the touch and permanent in color.

BENT ROCKERS The rockers of our rocking chairs are cut with the grain, and are then bent into shape by the use of steam pressure. This method has been adopted by us to avoid the danger of breaking incurred by the old way of cutting partly across the grain.

LEATHER For covering chairs, settles and table tops, we employ goat skins imported from Turkey, or where these are not large enough, carefully selected cow hides. The leather is tanned according to old-time methods, and we do not permit the use of injurious acids which impair the strength of the leather. After it has been rendered pliable by the tanning process, we treat the leather with dyes, staining it in soft dull tones in which two or more colors are blended.

CUSHIONS Our spring seat cushions for chairs and settles are built on steel bands securely fastened to wooden frames, a method of construction used for their cushions by nearly all automobile manufacturers, but original with us so far as furniture is concerned. These seat cushions are removable and slip easily into place; they are exceedingly comfortable, the cushions keep their shape and the leather lasts much longer than in a springless cushion. The back cushions are ventilated through air holes. When pressure is applied to the cushion the air is expelled; when relieved of pressure the cushion becomes filled with air, which penetrates the filling and keeps it from becoming matted.

HANDCRAFT METAL WORK Where hinges and pulls are needed upon our furniture, they are of handwrought copper, in simple design. The copper is hammered and then dulled and modulated in color by various processes until the soft tones of old metal are secured.

HANDCRAFT FOR HOMES The variety of our designs makes it possible for us to furnish houses of widely differing requirements. The small apartment, the large country house, or bungalow, the small house in town or country, have all received due consideration, and furniture especially appropriate to each is made in our Shops. For home-builders who wish complete harmony between woodwork and furniture, we provide stains for interior woodwork at a reasonable cost.

FOR PUBLIC BUILDINGS For public buildings, such as libraries, and for the club house, the cafe and the office, we build appropriate furniture and if desired, we furnish special drawings and estimates for pieces of special dimensions.

SHOPMARK Our Shopmark, the device of the Handscrew, will be found on every piece of Handcraft Furniture, and is a pledge of its excellence and durability, as well as a safeguard against imitators.

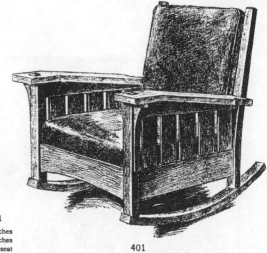

400 and 401

Height - 41 inches
Width - 27 inches
Spring cushion seat

400

401

432 and 433

Height - 41 inches
Width - 25½ inches
Spring cushion seat

432

433

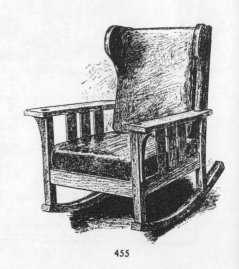

454 and 455

Height - 42½ inches
Width - 23¾ inches
Spring cushion seat

454

455

485

485
Height - 41½ inches
Width - 25½ inches
Spring cushion seat

499
Height - 41½ inches
Width - 26 inches
Spring cushion seat

499

427

426 and 427
Height - 42 inches
Width - 25½ inches
Spring cushion seat

426

460 and 461
Height - 42 inches
Width - 25½ inches
Spring cushion seat

461

460

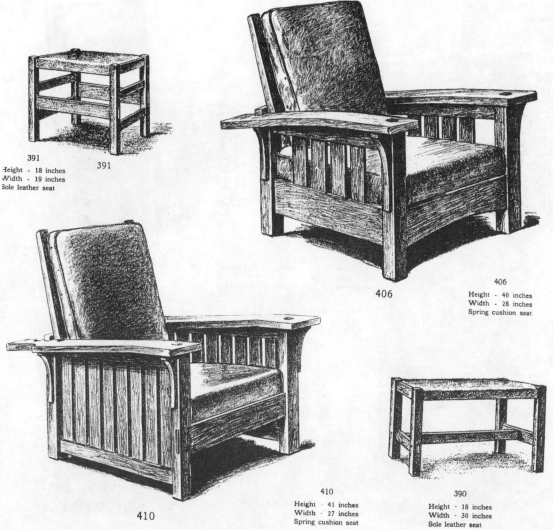

391

391

Height - 18 inches
Width - 19 inches
Sole leather seat

406

406

Height - 40 inches
Width - 28 inches
Spring cushion seat

410

410

Height - 41 inches
Width - 27 inches
Spring cushion seat

390

Height - 18 inches
Width - 30 inches
Sole leather seat

263

Height - 37 inches
Width - 72 inches
Depth - 25 inches
Spring cushion seat

413

413

Height - 39 inches
Width - 27½ inches
Stationary back
Spring cushion seat

412

412

Height - 40 inches
Width - 27 inches
Spring cushion seat

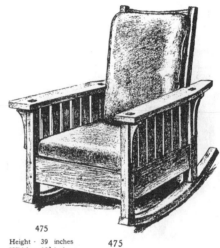

471

471

Height - 41 inches
Width - 25¾ inches
Spring cushion seat

475

475

Height - 39 inches
Width - 25¾ inches
Stationary back
Spring cushion seat

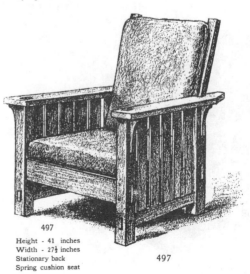

498

498

Height - 41 inches
Width - 27½ inches
Spring cushion seat

497

497

Height - 41 inches
Width - 27½ inches
Stationary back
Spring cushion seat

476

477

476 and 477
Height - 41 inches
Width - 22¾ inches
Spring cushion seat

411

411
Height - 41 inches
Width - 27½ inches
Stationary back
Spring cushion seat

470

470
Height - 41 inches
Width - 27½ inches
Spring cushion seat

830

830
Height - - 41 inches
Width - - 24¾ inches
Spring cushion seat

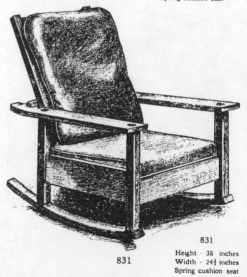

831

831
Height - 38 inches
Width - 24¾ inches
Spring cushion seat

810

810
Height - 39 inches
Width - 21¾ inches
Spring cushion seat

811

420

420 and 421
Height - 42 inches
Width - 25½ inches
Spring cushion seat

421

448

448 and 449
Height - 40 inches
Width - 24 inches
Spring cushion seat

449

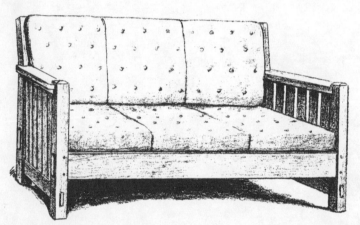

214
Height - 32½ inches
Width - 60 inches
Spring cushion seat

488 and 487
Height - 47 inches
Width - 24 inches
Spring cushion seat

488

487

446

447

446 and 447

Height - 40 inches
Width - 23¾ inches
Spring cushion seat

452

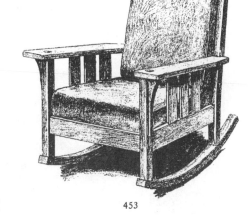

453

452 and 453

Height - 40 inches
Width - 23¾ inches
Spring cushion seat

422

423

422 and 423

Height - 38 inches
Width - 24 inches
Spring cushion seat

840

841

840 and 841
Height - 39½ inches
Width - 22¾ inches
Spring cushion seat

26 Smokers' Cabinet
Height, 29 in.
Top, 15 x 20 in.

26

25
Height - 22 inches
Width - 13½ inches
Depth - 13½ inches

24
Height - 28 inches
Width - 13½ inches
Depth - 13½ inches

828

829

828 and 829
Height - 37 inches
Width - 25¾ inches
Spring cushion seat

404

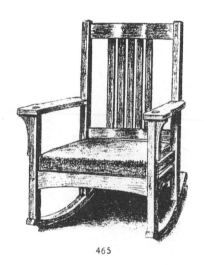

404 and 405
Height - 37 inches
Width - 22¾ inches
Spring cushion seat

405

464

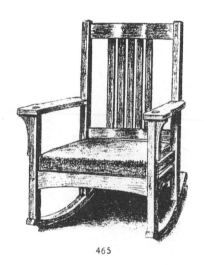

464 and 465
Height - 41 inches
Width - 22¾ inches
Spring cushion seat

465

466

466 and 467
Height - 41 inches
Width - 22¾ inches
Spring cushion seat

467

816

816 and 817
Height - 39½ inches
Width - 22¾ inches
Spring cushion seat

817

818

818 and 819
Height - 39½ inches
Width - 22¾ inches
Spring cushion seat

819

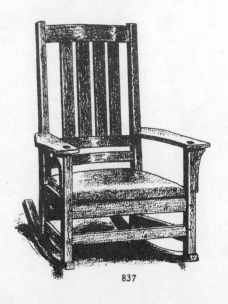

837

836 and 837
Height - 44 inches
Width - 22¾ inches
Spring cushion seat

836

822

823

822 and 823
Height - 36½ inches
Width - 23 inches
Spring cushion seat

820

558

821

820 and 821
Height - 36 inches
Width - 19½ inches
Spring cushion seat

558
Height - 17 inches
Top, 15 x 15 inches

559

225

559
Height - 20 inches
Top, 18 x 18 inches

225
Height - 36½ inches
Width - 48 inches
Depth - 20½ inches
Spring cushion seat

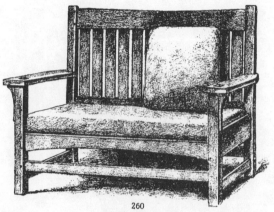

260

Height - 38½ inches
Width - 48 inches
Depth - 23 inches
Spring cushion seat

562

Height - 22 inches
Top, 20 x 20 inches

561

Height - 20 inches
Top, 18 x 18 inches

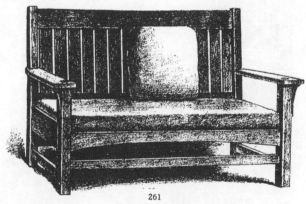

261

Height - 38½ inches
Width - 60 inches
Depth - 24 inches
Spring cushion seat

262

Height - 38½ inches
Width - 72 inches
Depth - 24 inches
Spring cushion seat

560

Height - 18 inches
Top, 16 x 16 inches

450 and 451

Height - 40 inches
Width - 24 inches
Spring cushion seat

450

451

436 and 437

Height - 40 inches
Width - 24 inches
Spring cushion seat

436

437

438 and 439

Height - 40 inches
Width - 24 inches
Spring cushion seat

439

438

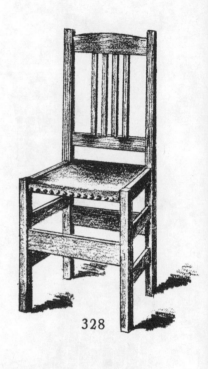

328

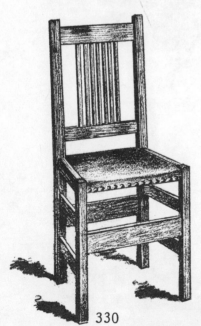

330

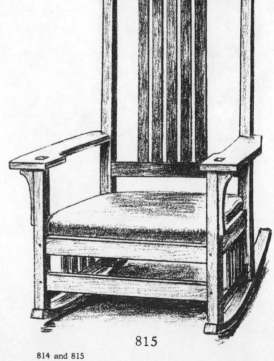

815

328 and 330
Height - 36½ inches
Width - 16½ inches
Sole leather seat

814 and 815
Height - 45½ inches
Width - 23 inches
Spring cushion seat

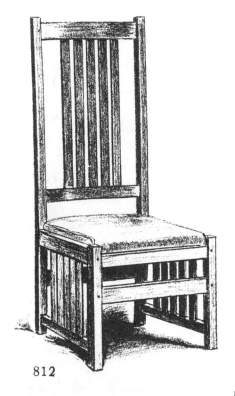

812

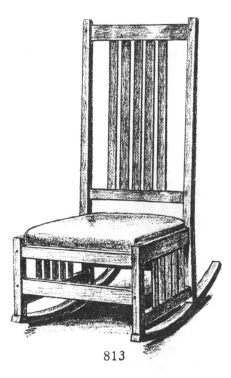

813

812 and 813
Height - 45 inches
Width - 19¼ inches
Spring cushion seat

224

224
Height - 45 inches
Width - 54 inches
Depth - 20 inches
Spring cushion seat

844

844 and 845
Height - 36½ inches
Width - 23 inches
Spring cushion seat

845

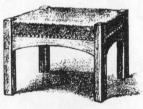

842 and 843
Height - 36 inches
Width - 19¾ inches
Spring cushion seat

842

843

394
Height - 16 inches
Width - 19¾ inches
Leather upholstered

227
Height - 36½ inches
Width - 48 inches
Depth - 20½ inches
Spring cushion seat

396
Height - 16 inches
Width - 20 inches
Leather upholstered

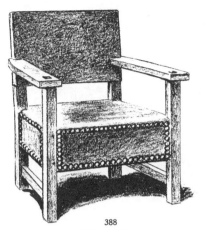

388

Height - 36 inches
Width - 24½ inches
Sole leather seat

388

Back view
Sole leather seat

384

Height - 34 inches
Width - 20 inches
Sole leather seat
To match arm chair
388

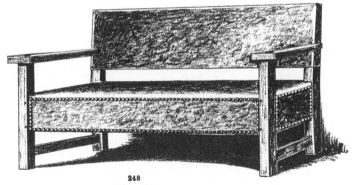

248

Height, 37 in.
Width, 70 in.
Depth, 24 in.
Sole leather seat
and back.

424

425

424 and 425

Height - 36½ inches
Width - 19½ inches
Spring cushion seat

515

Height - 24 inches
Top, 20 x 20 inches

826 and 827

Height - 36½ inches
Width - 23 inches
Spring cushion seat

826

827

824 and 825

Height - 36 inches
Width - 19¾ inches
Spring cushion seat

824

825

395

Height - 9 inches
Width - 19 inches
Leather upholstered

226

Height - 36½ inches
Width - 48 inches
Depth - 20½ inches
Spring cushion seat

354

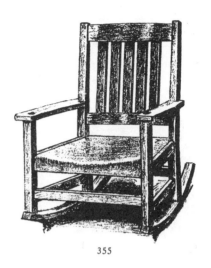

355

354 and 355
Height - 37 inches
Width - 23¾ inches
Sole leather seat

324
Height - 39 inches
Width - 21 inches
Leather upholstered
Slip seat

323
Height - 38 inches
Width - 18½ inches
Leather upholstered
Slip seat

360
Height - 36½ inches
Width - 18¼ inches
Sole leather seat

362
Height - 38½ inches
Width - 21¾ inches
Sole leather seat

332

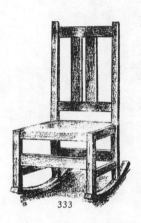

333

332 and 333
Height - 36 inches
Width - 17¾ inches
Sole leather seat

334

335

334 and 335
Height - 37½ inches
Width - 22½ inches
Sole leather seat

373

371

373
Height - 37½ inches
Width - 20¾ inches
Rush seat

371
Height - 35 inches
Width - 16¾ inches
Rush seat

344
Height - 37 inches
Width - 23 inches
Rush seat

343
Height - 36 inches
Width - 19¾ inches
Rush seat

343

341
Height - 36 inches
Width - 19¾ inches
Sole leather seat

342
Height - 38 inches
Width - 23 inches
Sole leather seat

364

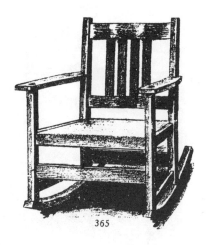

365

364 and 365
Height - 37½ inches
Width - 20¾ inches
Sole leather seat

352

353

352 and 353
Height - 37½ inches
Width - 20½ inches
Sole leather seat

549
Top, 48 inches in
diameter

350

351

350 and 351
Height - 35 inches
Width - 16¾ inches
Sole leather seat

244
Height - 37½ inches
Width - 39¼ inches
Depth - 19¼ inches
Sole leather seat

516
Top, 27 x 27 inches

846

847

846 and 847

Height - 36¼ inches
Width - 18¼ inches
Spring cushion seat

848

849

848 and 849

Height - 37¼ inches
Width - 21¾ inches
Spring cushion seat

838

839

838 and 839

Height - 37¼ inches
Width - 21¾ inches
Spring cushion seat

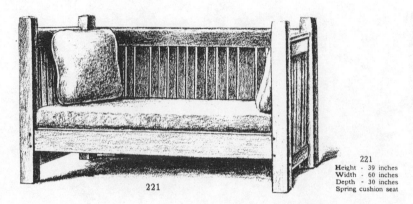

221
Height - 39 inches
Width - 60 inches
Depth - 30 inches
Spring cushion seat

221

222
Height - 39 inches
Width - 76 inches
Depth - 31 inches
Spring cushion seat

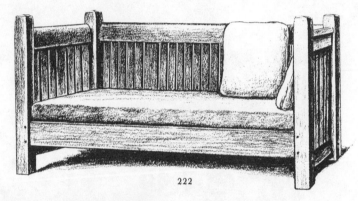

222

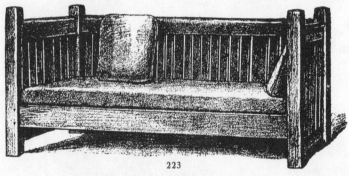

223
Height - 39 inches
Width - 84 inches
Depth - 32 inches
Spring cushion seat

223

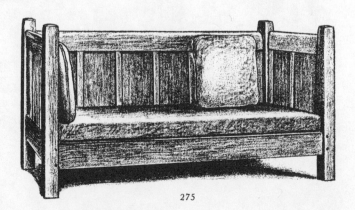

275
Height - 40 inches
Width - 84 inches
Depth - 32 inches
Spring cushion seat

275

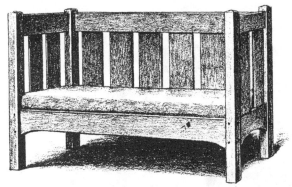

215

215
Height - 36 inches
Width - 54 inches
Depth - 24 inches
Spring cushion seat

216
Height - 36 inches
Width - 72 inches
Depth - 26 inches
Spring cushion seat

216

280

280
Height - 34 inches
Width - 60 inches
Depth - 30 inches
Spring cushion seat

281
Height - 34 inches
Width - 76 inches
Depth - 31 inches
Spring cushion seat

281

232
Height - 32½ inches
Width - 72 inches
Depth - 24 inches
Spring cushion seat

229
Height - 35 inches
Width - 72 inches
Depth - 26 inches
Spring cushion seat

264
Height - 34 inches
Width - 78 inches
Depth - 36 inches
This settle is shipped
knock down
Spring cushion seat

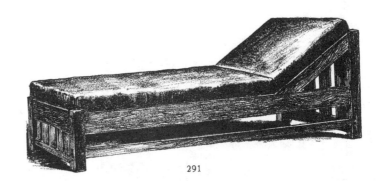

291
Height - 25½ inches
Width - 76 inches
Depth - 30 inches
Spring cushion seat

291

292
Height - 28 inches
Width - 80 inches
Depth - 30 inches
Spring cushion seat

292

293
Height - 28 inches
Width - 80 inches
Depth - 30 inches
Spring cushion seat

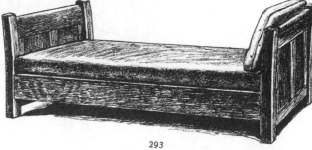

293

23
Height - 35½ inches
Top, 16 x 32 inches
With sliding copper
covered tray

509
Height - 24 inches
Top, 24 x 24 inches

217
Height - 30 inches
Width - 54 inches
Depth - 24 inches
Spring cushion seat

218
Height - 30 inches
Width - 72 inches
Depth - 26 inches
Spring cushion seat

233
Height - 26½ inches
Width - 72 inches
Depth - 24 inches
Spring cushion seat

233

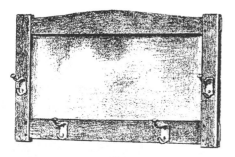

65

Size of glass
18 x 34 inches

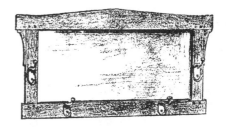

66

Size of glass
16 x 30 inches

95

Height - 29 inches
Width - 21½ inches
Depth - 12 inches

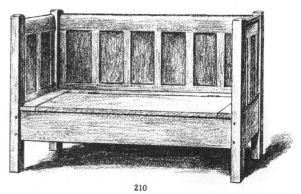

210

Height - 37 inches
Width - 54 inches
Depth - 20 inches

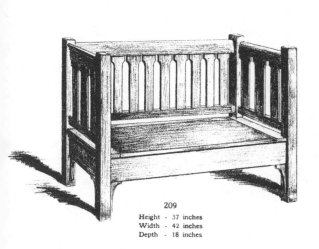

209

Height - 37 inches
Width - 42 inches
Depth - 18 inches

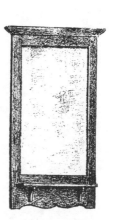

62

Size of glass, 14 x 24 inches

88

Height - 72 inches

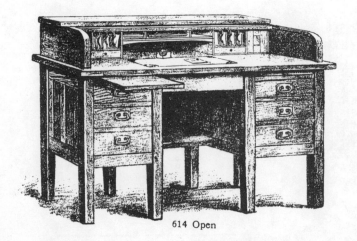

614 Open

614
Height - 39 inches
Top, 32 x 60 inches

352

851

614 Closed

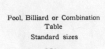

Pool, Billiard or Combination
Table
Standard sizes

851
Height - 42 inches
Width - 23 inches
Spring cushion seat

386
Height - 36 inches
Width - 19 inches
Sole leather seat

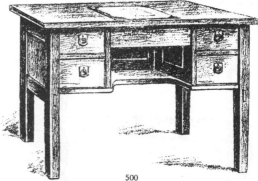

500
Top, 26 x 42 inches

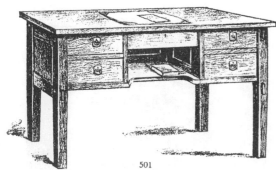

501
Top, 30 x 48 inches

387
Height - 38 inches
Width - 21 inches
Sole leather seat

850
Height - 38 inches
Width - 23 inches
Spring cushion seat

502
Top, 28 x 48 inches

601
Height - 34½ inches
Top, 20 x 34 inches

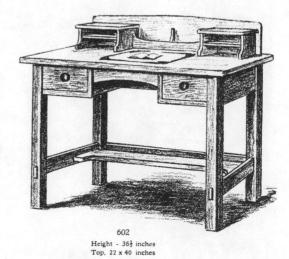

602
Height - 36½ inches
Top, 22 x 40 inches

613
Height - 40½ inches
Width - 31½ inches
Writing bed, 16½ x 30 inches

613

660

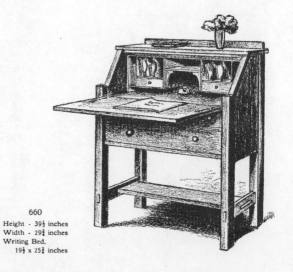

660
Height - 39½ inches
Width - 29¾ inches
Writing Bed,
19½ x 25¾ inches

610

Height - 38 inches
Top, 22 x 40 inches

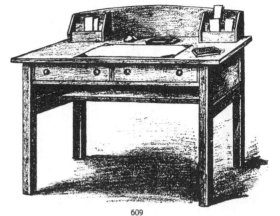

609

Height - 36½ inches
Top, 22 x 44 inches

22

Height - - - 28 inches
Top, 18 inches diameter
Wood, leather or copper top

615

Top, 32 x 60 inches

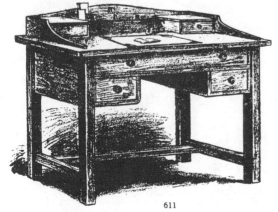

611

Height - 34 inches
Top, 22 x 44 inches

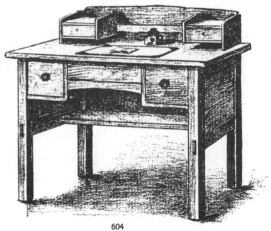

604

Height - 36½ inches
Top, 22 x 40 inches

645

Height - 55 inches
Width - 49 inches

646

Height - 55 inches
Width - 49 inches

648

647 and 648

Height - 55 inches
Width - 70 inches

536

Top, 24 inches in diameter

537

Top, 36 inches in diameter

647

642
Height - 55 inches
Width - 30 inches

641
Height - 55 inches
Width - 30 inches

642

641

644
Height - 55 inches
Width - 36 inches

643
Height - 55 inches
Width - 36 inches

644

643

598
Top, 30 x 48 inches

597
Top, 28 x 40 inches

597

538
Top, 30 inches in diameter

539
Top, 42 inches in diameter

542
Top, 36 inches in diameter

543   **543**
Top, 42 inches in diameter

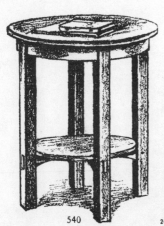

540   **540**
24 inches in diameter

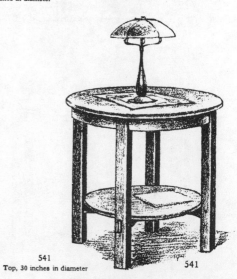

541   **541**
Top, 30 inches in diameter

45

45
Height - 45 inches
Width - 19 inches
Depth - 12 inches

46
Height - 42 inches
Width - 21 inches
Depth - 12 inches

46

80
Height - 22½ inches
Width - 30 inches
Depth - 8½ inches

47
Height - 42 inches
Width - 18 inches
Depth - 15 inches

47

52
Height - 28 inches
Top, 12 x 18 inches

52

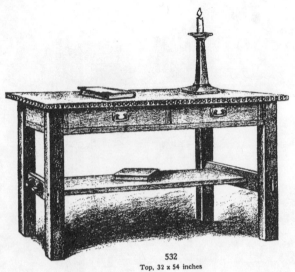

532
Top, 32 x 54 inches

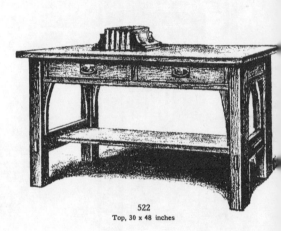

522
Top, 30 x 48 inches

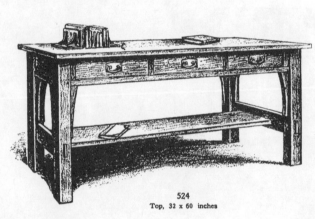

524
Top, 32 x 60 inches

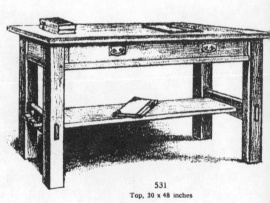

531
Top, 30 x 48 inches

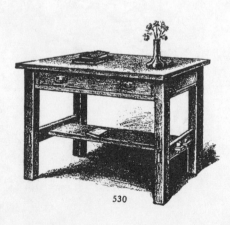

530

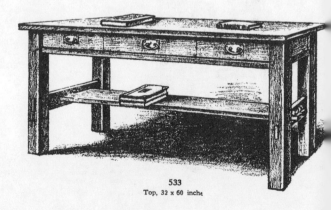

533
Top, 32 x 60 inches

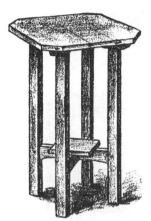

574
Top, 18 x 18 inches

576
Top, 24 x 24 inches

573
Top, 18 inches in diameter

577
Top, 30 inches in diameter

579
Top, 36 inches in diameter

578
Top, 30 x 30 inches

580
Top, 36 x 36 inches

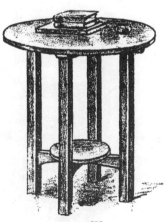

575
Top, 24 inches in diameter

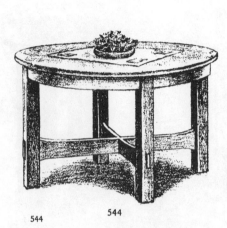

544

544

Top, 48 inches in
diameter

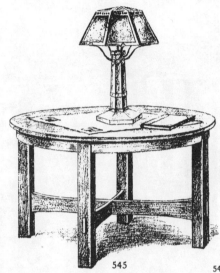

545

545

Top, 54 inches in
diameter

564

564
Top, 54 x 54 inches

Page 95

802

803

802 and 803
Height - 37½ inches
Width - 21¾ inches
Spring cushion seat

520
Top, 24 x 36 inches

520

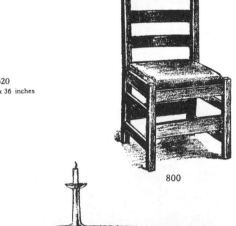

800

801

800 and 801
Height - 36½ inches
Width - 18½ inches
Spring cushion seat

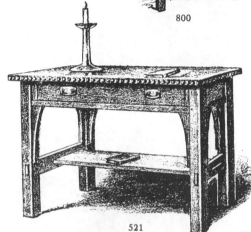

521
Top, 28 x 42 inches

521

593
Top, 30 x 48 inches

593

808 and 809
Height - 38½ inches
Width - 18½ inches
Spring cushion seat

808

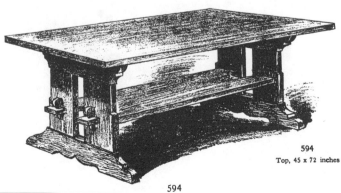

594
Top, 45 x 72 inches

594

809

211
Height - 22½ inches
Top, 16 x 40 inches

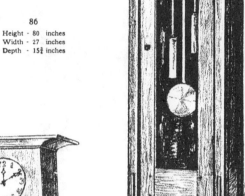

86
Height - 80 inches
Width - 27 inches
Depth - 15¾ inches

86

91

91
Height - 78 inches
Width - 19¼ inches
Depth - 12 inches

85

85
Height - 22 inches
Width - 16 inches
Depth - 8 inches

729

718

718
Top, 48, 54 and 60 inches
diameter
To extend 8, 10 and 12 feet

729
Height - 70 inches
Top, 17 x 50 inches

587
Height - 27 inches
Top, 16 x 16 inches

746
Height - 70 inches
Top, 16½ x 44 inches

719
Height - 65 inches
Top, 25⅝ x 38½ inches

508

508
Height - - 24 inches
Top, 24 inches diameter

507
Height - 24 inches
Top, 17 x 26 inches

761
Height - 60 inches
Top, 16 x 36 inches

708

708
Height - 44½ inches
Top, 20 x 48 inches

740 and 750
Height - 49 inches
Top, 22x48 inches

750

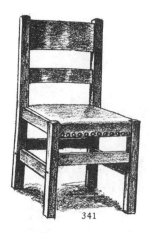

341

341
Height - 36 inches
Width - 19½ inches
Sole leather seat

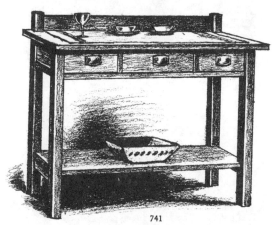

741
Height - 39½ inches
Top, 18 x 44 inches

707
Height - 43¾ inches
Top, 20 x 48 inches

332
Height - 36 inches
Width - 17¾ inches
Sole leather seat

332

343

343
Height - 36 inches
Width - 19¾ inches
Rush seat

740

745

745
Height - 48 inches
Top, 24 x 54 inches

546

546
Top 48 in. diameter
547
Same design
Top 42 in. diameter

717
Top, 48, 54 and 60 inches diameter
To extend 8, 10 and 12 feet
Non-dividing base

368

368
Height - 35 inches
Width - 16¾ inches
Sole leather seat

720

720
48, 54 and 60 inches
in diameter; to ex-
tend 8, 10 and 12 feet

737
Height - 62 inches
Top, 24 x 54 inches

372
Height - 37½ inches
Width - 20¾ inches
Rush seat

732
Height - 61¼ inches
Top, 25 x 72 inches

701

701
Height - 34¾ inches
Width - 21 inches

752
Height - 39¼ inches
Top, 15 x 40 inches

731
Height - 49¼ inches
Top, 25 x 72 inches

370
Height - 35 inches
Width - 16¾ inches
Rush seat

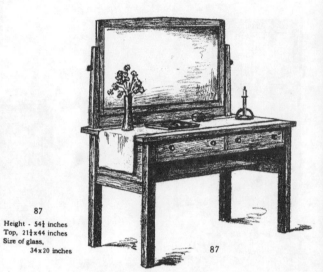

87
Height - 54½ inches
Top, 21½ x 44 inches
Size of glass,
34 x 20 inches

87

93
Height - 69 inches
Top, 22 x 48 inches
Size of glass,
34 x 28 inches

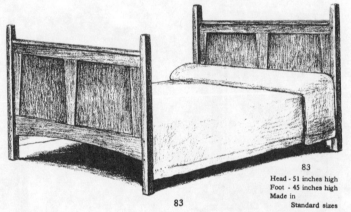

550
550
Top, 18 x 20 inches

83
83
Head - 51 inches high
Foot - 45 inches high
Made in
Standard sizes

98
Size of glass,
20 x 32 inches

97
Height - 40 inches
Top, 18 x 38 inches

98

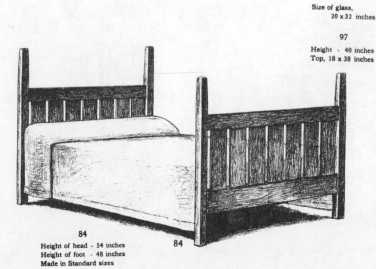

84
84
Height of head - 54 inches
Height of foot - 48 inches
Made in Standard sizes

97

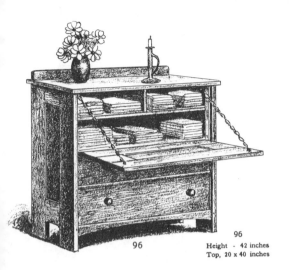

96

96
Height - 42 inches
Top, 20 x 40 inches

71

71
Height - 70 inches
Width of each panel,
22 inches

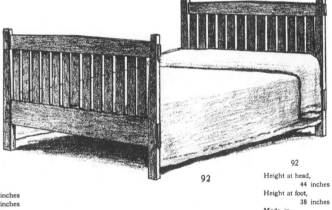

94

94
Height - 53 inches
Top, 19 x 39 inches

92

92
Height at head,
44 inches
Height at foot,
38 inches
Made in
Standard sizes

100
Size of glass, 40 x 20 inches

99
Height - 38 inches
Top, 22 x 48 inches

100

70
Height - 70 inches
Width of each panel,
22 inches

70

99

THE WORK OF L. & J.G. STICKLEY

After 1912 when L. & J. G. Stickley changed their red Hand-craft Furniture decal to a white decal with "The Work of L. & J. G. Stickley" in a rectangle and later still to a branded signature, the line was fully developed. The advertising plates shown in this section are from this period. We have displayed here some examples that appeared in the familiar and reprinted catalogue "The Work of L. & J. G. Stickley." Other models never shown before, limited production items and other interesting original designs, are also shown here. Some style numbers and sizes were not shown on the original illustrations. This material was assembled from drawings and plates furnished by Alfred Audi of Fayetteville, N.Y.

THE WORK OF L&J.G.STICKLEY

FAYETTEVILLE NEW YORK U.S.A.

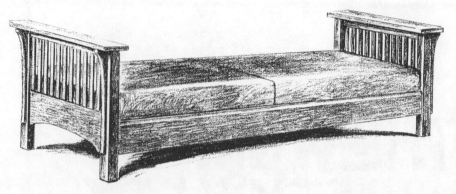

296 Couch
Height 16 in.
Width 86 in. over all
Depth 30 in. over all
Spring cushion seat

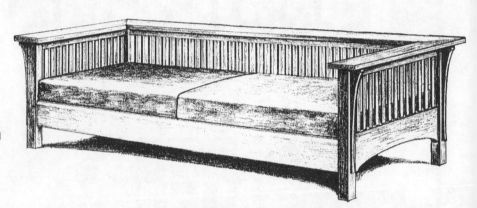

234 Settle
Height 25½in.
Width 86in. over all
Depth 34in. over all
Spring cushion seat

220 Settle
Height 29in.
Width 84½in. over all.
Depth 36¾in. over all.
Spring cushion seat

416 Arm Chair
Height 27in.
Width 39in. over all
Depth 35in. over all
Spring cushion seat

14069-6 Arm Chair

14069-5 Arm Rocker

14069-8 Settle

295 Couch
Height 22in.
Depth 28in.
Spring cushion seat

265 Settle

Couch
Height 28 in.
Width 80 in.
Depth 30 in.
Spring cushion seat

428 Chair
Height 30in.
Width   28in.
Spring cushion seat

429 Rocker
To match 428 Chair

232 Settle
28"H 72"W 27"D

744 Settle

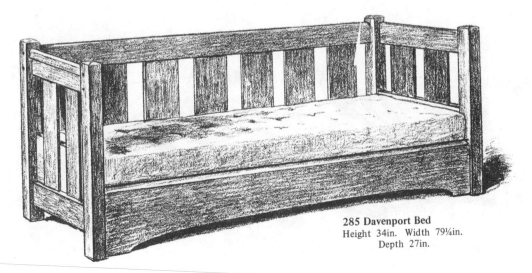

285 Davenport Bed
Height 34in. Width 79¼in.
Depth 27in.

397 Stool
Height 16in. Width 20in
Spring cushion seat

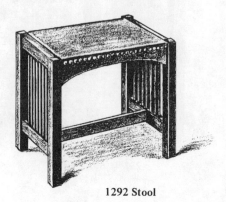

1292 Stool

398 Stool

389 Stool
Height 15½in. Width 21in.
Spring cushion seat

399 Stool

393 Stool

751 Arm Rocker

751½ Arm Rocker

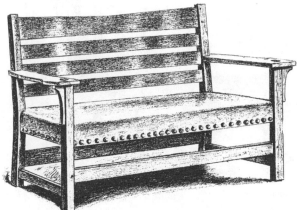

235 Settle

554 Tabourette
Height 16in.
Top 12x12in.

450 and 451
Height 40in. Width 24in.
Spring cushion seat

450 Arm Chair

451 Arm Rocker

1322 Dining Arm Chair

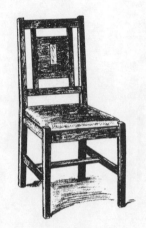

1320 Dining Chair

330 Dining Chair

658 Dining Arm Chair

657 Dining Chair

1265 Rocker

1263 Arm Rocker

346 Dining Chair

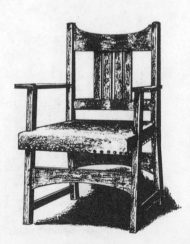

348 Dining Arm Chair

1358 Dining Arm Chair

334 Dining Arm Chair

1356 Dining Chair

332 Dining Chair

346 Dining Chair

333 Rocker

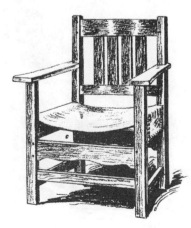

336 Dining Arm Chair

348 Dining Arm Chair

480 Arm Chair
Height 38in. Width 25in.
Spring cushion seat and back

1420 Arm Chair

482

483

**482 Arm Chair and
483 Arm Rocker**
Height 39½in. Width 27½in.
Spring cushion seat and back

402 Arm Chair

403 Arm Rocker

61 Hall Glass
Center glass 18 x 28 in.
Side glasses 10 x 18 in.
Size of frame 24½ x 55½ in.

89 Costumer
Height 72 in.

208 Hall Seat
Height 34 in.
Width 54 in.
Depth 18 in.
Drawer under seat.

60 Hall Glass
Glass 18 x 33 in.
Size of frame 25¾ x 46¼in.

82 Costumer
Height 72 in.

207 Hall Seat
Height 32 in.
Width 42 in.
Depth 18 in.
Drawer under seat.

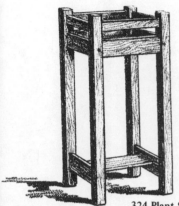

324 Plant Stand
Height 28 in.
Width 13½ in.
Depth 13½ in.

325 Plant Stand
Height 22 in.
Width 13½ in.
Depth 13½ in.

583 Tabourette

510 Tabourette

512 Table

Nest of Tables

1301 Dining Arm Chair

1267 Arm Rocker

1201 Dining Arm Chair

1200 Dining Chair

328 Dining Chair

1300 Dining Chair

14069-3 Arm Rocker

1260 Dining Arm Chair

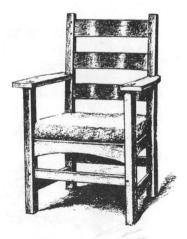

14069-4 Dining Arm Chair

Table

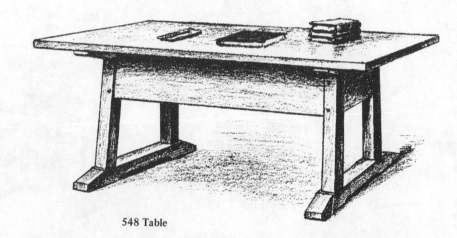

548 Table

511 Table
36 x 72 in.

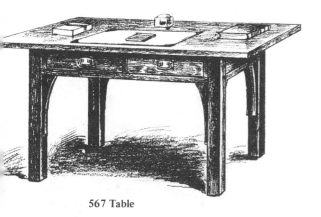

567 Table

512 Desk Table

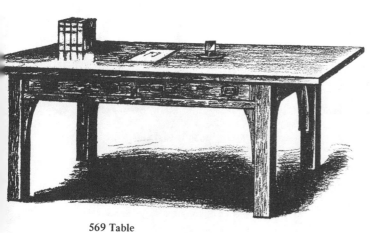

569 Table

Table

568 Table

565 Table

643 Book Case
Height 55 in.
Width 36 in.
Two doors

652 Book Case
Height 51¼ in.
Width 22in.

1282 Table

650 Book Case

651 Book Case

Book Stand
Height 36 in.
Width 28 in.

599 Table
Height 29 in.
Top 42 x 84 in.

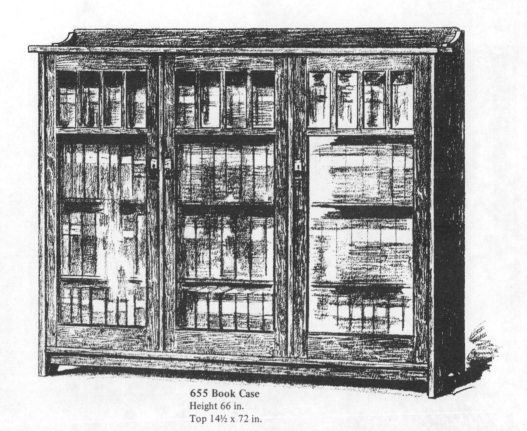

655 Book Case
Height 66 in.
Top 14½ x 72 in.

653 Book Case
Height 55 in.
Width at top 27 in.

654 Book Case
Height 55 in.
Width at top 50 in.

637 Book Case
Height 48 in.
Top 13½ x 36 in.

638 Book Case
Same design as 637
Top 13½ x 48 in.

639 Book Case
Height 48 in.
Top 13½ x 60 in.

656 Book Case
Height 66 in.
Top 14½ x 72 in.

657 Book Case
Height 66 in.
Top 14½ x 26 in.

572 Checker Table
Height 29 in.
Top 30 x 30 in.
Checkers, mahogany
and maple.

529 Table
Top 28 x 42 in.
One drawer

583 Lunch Table
Height 30 in.
Diameter 30 in.

612 Desk
Height 36¼ in.
Top 30 x 48 in.

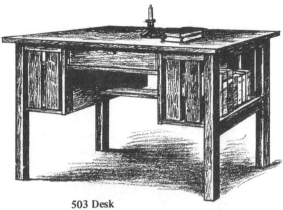

503 Desk
Height 30 in.
Top 28 x 42 in.

402 Desk

604 Desk
Height 36¼ in.
Top 22 x 40 in.

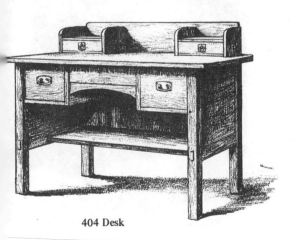

404 Desk

611 Desk
Height 34¾ in.
Top 26 x 42

21 Ash Tray Stand
Height 22 in.
Top 10 x 10 in.

27 Pedestal
Height 36 in.
Top 12 x 12 in.
28 Pedestal
Same design as 27
Height 42 in.
Top 13 x 13 in.

20 Waste Basket
Height 16 in.
Size at top 13 x 13 in.

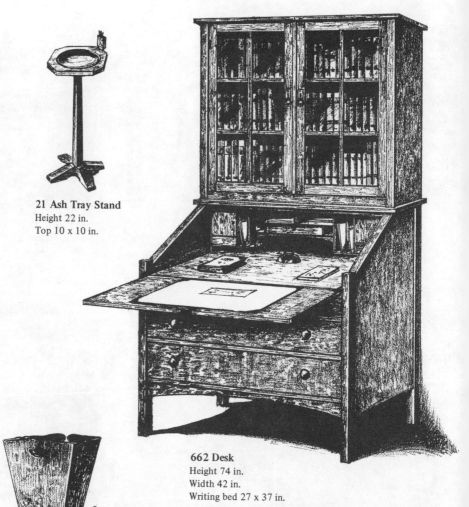

662 Desk
Height 74 in.
Width 42 in.
Writing bed 27 x 37 in.

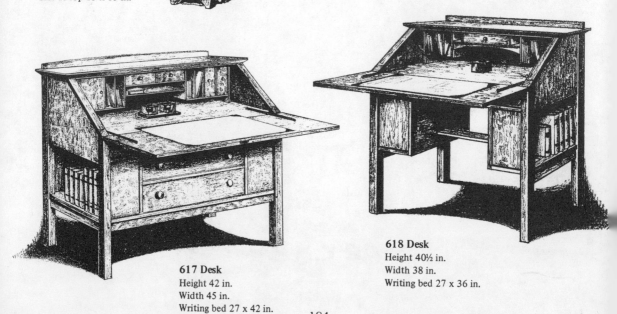

617 Desk
Height 42 in.
Width 45 in.
Writing bed 27 x 42 in.

618 Desk
Height 40½ in.
Width 38 in.
Writing bed 27 x 36 in.

661 Desk Closed

661 Desk
Height 44½ in.
Width 42 in.
Writing bed 27 x 37 in.

661 Desk   Open

Desk Closed

Desk Open

Desk Open

Desk Closed

600 Desk
Height 30 in.
Top 32 x 60 in.

683 Table Desk
Height 30 in.
Top 24 x 36 in.

850 Office Chair
Height 38 in.
Width 23 in.
Spring cushion seat

614 Roll Top Desk
Height 43 in.
Top 34 x 60 in.

518 Table Desk
Height 30 in.
Top 24 x 36 in.

400 Desk

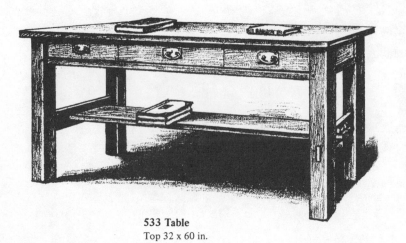

533 Table
Top 32 x 60 in.

508 Tea Table
Height 24 in.
Diameter 24 in.

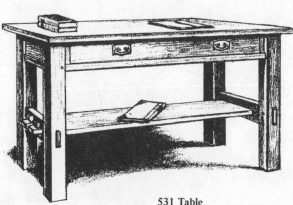

531 Table
Same design as 530
Top 30 x 48 in.
One drawer

588 Tip Table
Height 28¼ in.
Top 28 x 28 in.

589 Tip Table
Height 24 in.
Diameter 20 in.

530 Table
Top 24 x 36 in.

599 Table
Height 29 in.
Top 32 x 60
Also made 32 x 54 in.

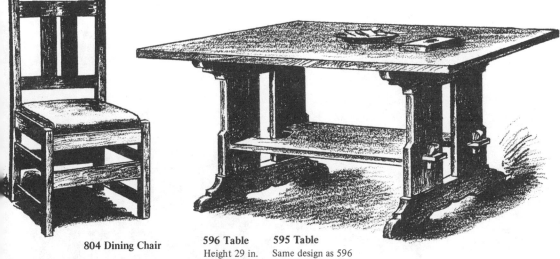

804 Dining Chair

596 Table
Height 29 in.
Top 36 x 60

595 Table
Same design as 596
Top 36 x 54 in.

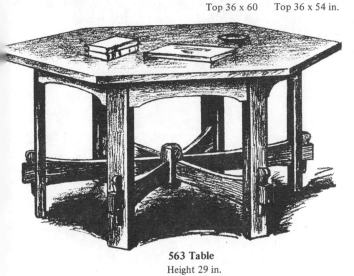

563 Table
Height 29 in.
Top 48 x 48 in.

41 Magazine Stand
Height 42 in.
Width 21 in.

727 China Closet
Height 55 in.
Width 34 in.
Depth 15 in.

582 Table
Height 29 in.
Top 42 x 42 in.

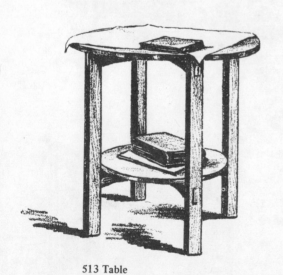

513 Table

728 China Closet
Height 55 in.
Width 48 in.
Depth 15 in.

Sideboard
Height 76 in.
Lenght 12 ft.

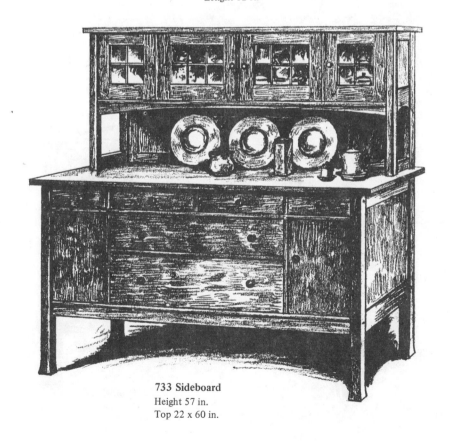

733 Sideboard
Height 57 in.
Top 22 x 60 in.

711 Sideboard
Height 46 in.
Top 22 x 60 in.

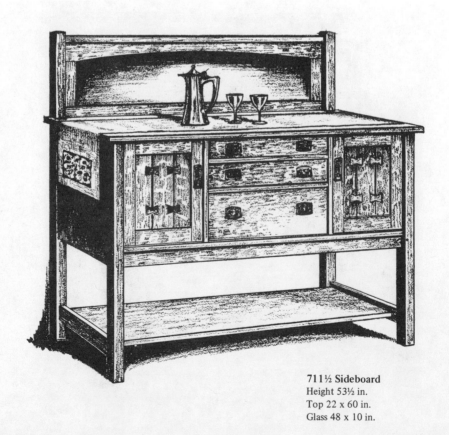

711½ Sideboard
Height 53½ in.
Top 22 x 60 in.
Glass 48 x 10 in.

Sideboard
Top 22 x 60 in.

736 Sideboard
Height 48 in.
Top 22 x 66 in.

735 Sideboard
Same design as 736
Height 46 in.
Top 22 x 56 in.

507 Tea Table
Height 24 in.
Top 17 x 26

China Closet

722 Dining Table
Diameter 48 in.
To extend 6 and 8 ft.

713 Dining Table
Diameter 48 and 54 in.
To extend 8, 10 and 12 ft.

422 Arm Chair

551 Drop Leaf Table
Height 30 in.
Top Open 48 x 48 in.
With leaves down 16 x 48 in.

553 Drop Leaf Table
Height 30 in.
Diameter of top open 42 in.
With leaves down 14 x 42 in.

552 Drop Leaf Table
Height 30 in.
Top open 42 x 42 in.
With leaves down 14 x 42 in.

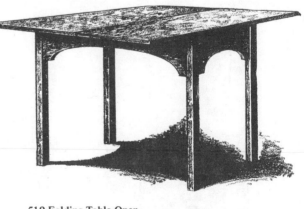

519 Folding Table Closed
Height 30 in.
Top 18 x 36 in.

519 Folding Table Open
Height 30 in.
Top 36 x 36

743½ Sideboard
Height 49 in.
Top 20 x 48 in.
Glass 38 x 10 in.

958 Dining Arm Chair
Height 19¾ in.
Width 19¾ in.
Wood Seat

735½ Sideboard
Height 50 in.
Top 22 x 56 in.
Glass 44 × 10 in.

736½ Sideboard
Height 50 in.
Top 22 x 66 in.
Glass 52 x 10 in.

743 Sideboard
Height 43 in.
Top 20 x 48 in.

956 Dining Chair
Height 35 in.
Width 16¾ in.
Wood Seat

709½ Sideboard
Height 50½ in.
Top 22 x 54 in.
Glass 44 x 10 in.

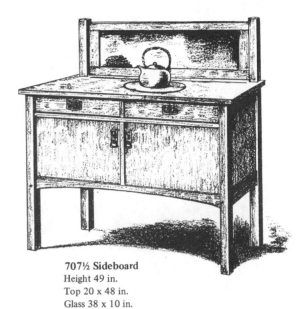

707½ Sideboard
Height 49 in.
Top 20 x 48 in.
Glass 38 x 10 in.

1342½ Dining Arm Chair
Height 37½ in.
Width 21¾ in.
Leather upholstered seat

Serving Table

734 Sideboard
Height 44 in.
Top 20 x 48 in.

942 Arm Chair
Height 37½ in.
Width 21¾ in.
Wood Seat

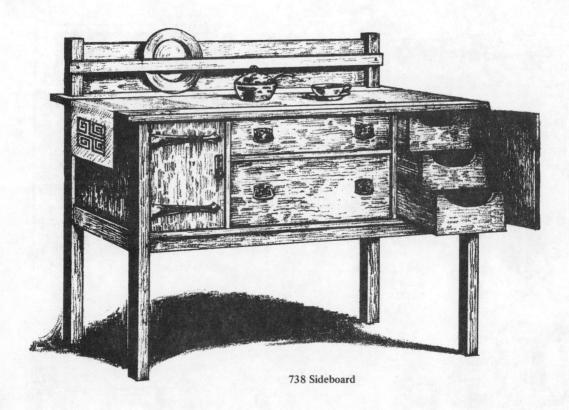

738 Sideboard

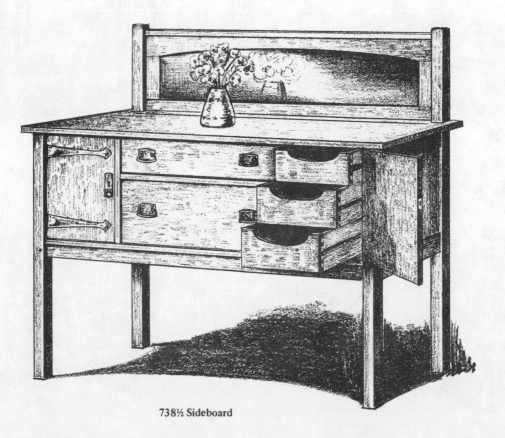

738½ Sideboard

Sideboard
Height 48 in.
Top 20 x 48 in.

Sideboard

748 Sideboard
Height 48 in.
Top 22 x 54 in.

748½ Sideboard
Height 51⅓ in.
Top 22 x 54 in.
Glass 44 x 10 in.

742 Sideboard
Height 48 in.
Top 18 x 44 in.

742½ Sideboard
Height 47 in.
Top 18 x 44 in.
Glass 32 x 8 in.

747 Serving Table
Height 44 in.
Top 20 x 48 in.

747½ Serving Table
Height 49½ in.
Top 20 x 48 in.
Glass 38 x 10 in.

1342 Dining Arm Chair
Height 37½ in.
Width 21¾ in.
Flag seat

1352 Dining Arm Chair
Height 37½ in.
Width 20¾ in.
Flag seat

1350 Dining Chair
Height 35 in.
Width 16¾ in.
Flag seat

744 Serving Table
Height 44½ in.
Top 20 x 54 in.

744½ Serving Table
Height 50 in.
Top 20 x 54 in.
Glass 44 x 10 in.

102 Chiffonier
Height 50 in.
Top 18 x 36 in.

111 Chiffonier
Height 48 in.
Top 19 x 40 in.

112 Closed

112 Open

112 Wardrobe
Height 60 in.
Top 22½ x 50 in.

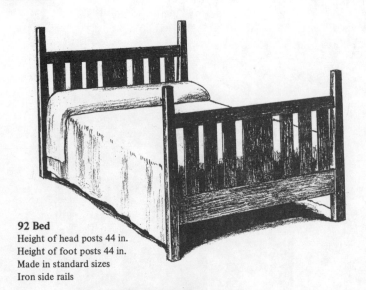

92 Bed
Height of head posts 44 in.
Height of foot posts 44 in.
Made in standard sizes
Iron side rails

81 Dresser
Height 67 in.
Top 21 x 44 in.
Glass 24 x 30 in.

99 Chest of Drawers
Height 38 in.
Top 22 x 40 in.

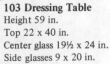

103 Dressing Table
Height 59 in.
Top 22 x 40 in.
Center glass 19½ x 24 in.
Side glasses 9 x 20 in.

115 Bed
Height of head posts 54 in.
Height of foot posts 48 in.
Made in standard sizes
Iron side rails

77 Dresser
Height 69¼ in.
Top 18¼ x 24 in.
Glass 16 x 24 in.

101 Dresser
Height 68 in.
Top 22 x 54 in.
Glass 28 x 45

110 Stand
Height 29 in.
Top 14 x 18 in.

114 Bed
Height of head 44 in.
Height of foot 38 in.
Made in standard sizes
Iron siderails

105 Stand
Height 29½ in.
Top 14 x 20 in.

106 Chest of Drawers
Height 36 in.
Top 22 x 54 in.

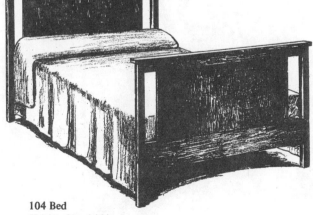

104 Bed
Height of head 46 in.
Height of foot 38 in.
Made in standard sizes
Iron siderails

551 Serving Table
Height 29 in.
Top closed 16 x 20 in.
Top open 16 x 44 in.
Top drawer fitted with
cedar tray

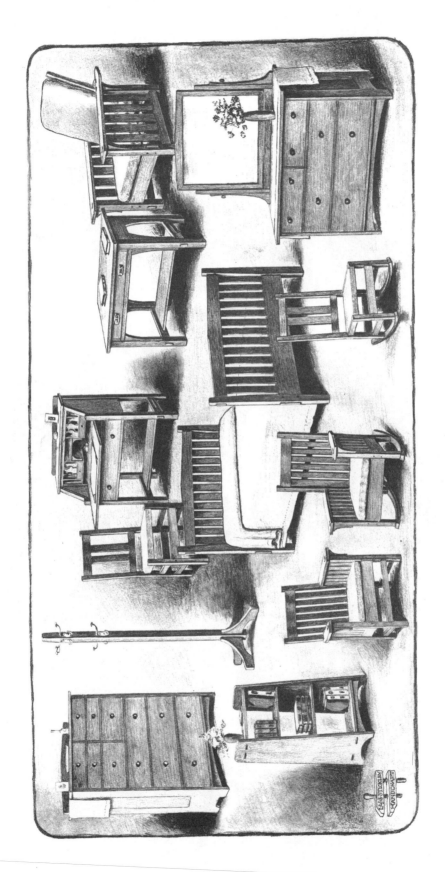

Oak sideboard from the Onandaga Shops of L. & J. G. Stickley, circa 1905.
From the collection of Stephen Gray.

Oak Magazine Stand from the Onandaga Shops of L. & J. G. Stickley, circa 1905.
From the collection of Stephen Gray.

THE WORK OF
L.&J.G. STICKLEY

142
174